THE STRUCTURE OF THE NOVEL

CONTENTS

THE STRUCTURE OF THE NOVEL

I

NOVELS OF ACTION AND CHARACTER

THE object of this book is to study the principles of structure in the novel. Those principles, it is obvious, cannot be located in any one example of fiction, however great. The method I shall employ, therefore, is the following. I shall divide the novel into a few rough and ready but easily recognisable classes; I shall consider not merely one kind of structure but several, discover if possible the laws which operate in each, and find an æsthetic justification for those laws. In all their manifestations, I shall then try to show, those laws spring from a common necessity and postulate a general principle.

Before plunging into the subject, however, it

will be best to limit our area by indicating what lies beyond it.   In recent years three interesting books on the novel have appeared.   They touch upon fascinating aspects of the subject and they are by writers of individual talent.   *The Craft of Fiction*, by Mr Percy Lubbock, is concerned chiefly with "form"; but though the author says many good things, he does not quite divulge what form is: it is clear, however, that he means by it something different from what is meant here by structure.   Form, as he conceives it, is evidently dependent on what he calls "the point of view," and consists in the writer's maintaining a severely limited, narrow, and undeviating attitude to his theme, as Henry James does for example.   Mr Lubbock deals with a specific type of structure, then, rather than with structure in general.   Mr E. M. Forster follows with *Aspects of the Novel*.   Mr Forster does not hold much with form; he sees no reason why a novel should stick to one "point of view"; he is content so long as the novelist "bounces" us into a belief in his characters and gives us "life."   Last of all appears Mr John Carruthers with his packed little essay, *Scheherazade; or The Future of the English Novel,* proving that the novel must have form because Professor Whitehead says that life has it. Nineteenth-century materialism, with its denial of purpose, he maintains, is outmoded; we must believe now in "organic purpose." According to this, life has a pattern; therefore a novel must have a pattern. The novelist of the future "will have rid himself of the false beliefs oppressing the novelists of to-day, that the wholeness of things is ' not theirs in life,' and that all attempts to achieve wholeness in art must remain at best a sort of pretty-pretty deception. He will believe instead that in shaping his creation into an organic pattern he is working in the very spirit of life itself, and that the 'globed compacted things' he makes contain the same kind of reality, the same kind of truth, as he can find all round him in the world of hard, unadulterate fact. He will know that he selects only in order to reveal what *is*."

Of these three writers the one who keeps his eye most vigilantly on the object is Mr Lubbock. He is narrow, it is true; to please him the road

must wind uphill all the way; and the more difficult it is the better; difficulty in a novel becomes
to him, one might almost say, an additional
source of æsthetic enjoyment. But he has the
rare merit of being concerned with the novel as
a specific form of art, not merely as one of the
manifestations of life. There is a pattern in life,
he would no doubt agree with Mr Carruthers,
but he appreciates the fact that there is a difference between it and the pattern of a novel. The
novel must give us "life," he would admit with
Mr Forster, but what is life? he might ask, and
what is the difference between life as we live
it and life as we see it in Thackeray or in
Henry James? In short, in a work on the novel
he remembers the novel. Mr Forster argues
that the novel must give us life because life
does; Mr Carruthers maintains that the novel
must present a pattern because life does. Both,
no doubt, are right: what they forget is the
novel.

To remember the novel the first thing one must
do is to assume (that is, forget) such things as
that it is about life and that life has a pattern.
After all, the fact that the novelist writes about

life is not so very extraordinary; it is the only thing he knows anything about. Nor is it surprising that he should inevitably dispose life in a pattern when he writes, no matter what he may think of it. He does so because he makes a statement, and life does not. In that statement he may say that life is a chaos, or that life is an order; but unless he writes like Miss Gertrude Stein, the statement at any rate will be clear, and clearer than life. The point is obvious enough. We never think of complaining that Birmingham or Clapham has no form, or that Smith's life is without design; but we would complain if even the most mediocre novel about Birmingham or Smith had not some approach to coherence. It is axiomatic that the pattern of no novel, however formless, can ever be so formless as life as we see it; for even *Ulysses* is less confusing than Dublin. What Mr Carruthers really wants the novel to live up to is a new philosophical conception of the universe, not its own laws. New philosophical conceptions may no doubt be of use to the novelist; they may help him to see the world more completely; and ideally they should be part of his knowledge. But however long he listens to them, they will not tell him what the laws of the novel are. He may write a novel structurally good, imagining that life is a chaos, and one structurally false, thinking it an order.

The reason for this is that the laws of the novel, the laws of imaginative creation in prose, are not within his control. He may not know them; all that matters is that he should observe them. Theories about them may help him, or hinder him; and ignorance equally. If he modifies those laws consciously to his purpose, as James did, he is likely to narrow them; if, like Dickens, he knows little or nothing about them, he will go on writing with equal enthusiasm whether he is observing them or not. Nothing, however clever, that he may do to them can modify them essentially. The Jamesian novel is not a resumption or a fulfilment of the previous tradition, or an improvement on it, but a minor offshoot. *The Ambassadors* does not supersede *Wuthering Heights*; it is in a tradition exactly as important as its author, and a great novel is always in a tradition greater than that of any author. The danger of a practising theorist on the novel like James is that he ends by doing exactly what he wants to do. He excludes three-quarters of life where another would make some effort to subdue it. His plots will no doubt be very neat; but they will not have the organic movement, the ebb and flow, of a plot in the main tradition. They will be quite without those "formidable erosions of contour" which Mr Forster, quoting Nietzsche, admires so much. "All that is prearranged is false," Mr Forster ends by exclaiming. There could not be a better criticism of the Jamesian novel.

Nevertheless, the novel is rich in offshoots, and these are of considerable secondary importance. They include some of the works of Flaubert and James. The fate of such novels follows a general course. At first they are accepted by the few as the last word in fiction, as the best and newest form. Then they fall into their place, and are absorbed into the tradition as minor elements. They add something to it which remains there for general use.

Having admitted the value of those offshoots, however, we may leave them; for the purpose of this book is to trace the general and given structure of the novel rather than the many interesting varieties of form which have evolved from it. Many of those forms are controversial still, and I wish to remain as far as is practicable outside controversy. As instances of works controversial directly or indirectly, Mr Lubbock's book and Mr Carruthers' may serve very well. To Mr Lubbock certain forms of the novel are good and others bad, and the best of all is that which was used by Henry James. To Mr Carruthers all novels, no matter what their subject-matter, their aim, or their style, should have a clear and definite pattern. I shall start with the assumption that all the main forms of the novel are good: those whose pattern is definite, those whose pattern is vague; those which proceed by strict development, those which seem to have hardly any development at all. I shall not enter into the present controversy; I shall try rather to contribute a few general considerations which should be relevant to it.

The first difficulty is that almost all the terms which it is usual to apply to the novel at present are controversial or semi-controversial.

I mean such terms as "pattern," "rhythm," "surface," "point of view," and so on. It is customary, for example, to find pattern in Henry James, and whenever a critic uses the word he is putting in an indirect plea for the Jamesian novel. Mr Forster finds "pattern," inevitably enough, in *The Ambassadors*, and "rhythm," more originally, in Marcel Proust. Mr Lubbock, again, quite fails to find his "point of view" in Tolstoy, and is somewhat dismayed. There is something a little precious in writing about the novel in this way. We assent lazily to those terms, but we do not really believe that a novel has a pattern like a carpet or a rhythm like a tune. When Mr Forster mentions "pattern" and "rhythm" we know what he is talking about, but we know, too, that it is neither pattern nor rhythm. James is the father of most of those question-begging terms; he was an incurable impressionist; and he has infected criticism with his vocabulary of hints and nods. Applied to works of the first rank, that vocabulary is ridiculously inadequate. "Pattern" may suffice quite well for *The Ambassadors*; "rhythm" is incapable of indicating the quality of Proust. It sentimentalises him, as it would sentimentalise any really first-rate novelist. In the same way it would be obviously absurd to speak of the "pattern" of *Crime and Punishment*, though it has a pattern, or of the "surface" of *Tom Jones*, though its surface is admirable. Criticism tacitly admits this by never attempting to do so.

The term "plot" stands outside these dangers. It is a definite term, it is a literary term, and it is universally applicable. It can be used in the widest popular sense. It designates for everyone, not merely for the critic, the chain of events in a story and the principle which knits it together. It covers *Treasure Island* and *Tristram Shandy*, *Wuthering Heights* and *The Ambassadors*, *The Three Musketeers* and *Ulysses*. In all these novels a few things happen, and in a certain order, and in every novel things must happen and in a certain order. As they must needs happen, however, it is the order which distinguishes one kind of plot from another. Events move along one line in *Treasure Island*, along another in *Vanity Fair*. This volume will be more specifically, then, a study of some of the lines along which events move in the novel; in other words, a survey of some of the main plots, each with its interior principle, which the novel has used. My concern will not be at all with what those plots "should be," but simply with what they are. The only thing which can tell us about the novel is the novel.

The most simple form of prose fiction is the story which records a succession of events, generally marvellous. *The Famous History of Doctor Faustus* is a good example, and the best indication of what it sets out to do is given in its full title: "A discourse of the most famous Doctor John Faustus of Wittenberg in Germany, Conjurer and Necromancer; wherein is declared many strange things that himself had seen and done in the earth and air, with his bringing up, his travels, studies, and last end." As the advertisement announces, the story appeals chiefly to our irresponsible curiosity. It is one of those books which, as Mr Forster says, can only keep us going by "and then—and then." We are not interested in Dr Faustus, but only in what is going to happen. That, moreover, is sure to be surprising, for it may be anything at all: Faustus may be taken down to see Hell by Mephistopheles, or may fly from Wittenberg to Munich. Neither the actions nor the places have any strict relation to one another; the events may occur in any order, and Hell has the same kind of geographical reality as Leipzig or Venice. The only scene which could not have been in any other position is Faustus's death and descent into Hell in the last chapter. In the action, in short, the writer is freely and continuously satisfying his desire for the marvellous all the time; and it is this that gives the book its naïve charm. The action is a perpetual "escape."

This charm, however, could never be recaptured by even a moderately sophisticated writer, and it has never been recaptured by any one since the triumph of the novel. It depends on the absence of plot, on arbitrary, not on ordered, freedom; and with the advent of plot, with the novel, it had to go. But there is a form of the novel which sets out to do something as naïve as *The History of Doctor Faustus* does. This form works within stricter limitations, with greater skill, and with considerably less sincerity. This, as it is the simplest, the most popular, and least considerable form of the novel, may serve best as an introduction to the more important divisions.

I mean, of course, the "romance." Its object, as that of *Doctor Faustus*, is to arouse our curiosity. But curiosity is obviously greatly intensified if the events follow a line; if instead of asking for another marvel the reader is made to wonder what is going to happen next. By substituting a sequence for a string of happenings, by making a single complicated action take the place of a succession of actions, the story-teller is able to evoke a whole new scale of more poignant emotions: anticipation, apprehension, fear, and the like. Having aroused them, however, he has, if he is to continue to delight the reader, to give some assurance that they will be allayed again. *Doctor Faustus*, as it pleased the reader uniformly by its mere succession of events, could afford to end unhappily; the romance, the novel of action, as it makes the reader suffer occasionally, and as its chief object is to please, must end happily. We can only enjoy the dangers through which the hero passes with the complete irresponsibility with which we enjoy the episodes in *Doctor Faustus*, because we know he will escape in the end. There are novels in which the hero is not permitted to escape; but these are never concerned primarily or alone with action, they arouse feelings of a more complex kind than curiosity, apprehension or final confidence, and the pleasure which they give us is not that of simple story-telling.

Irresponsible delight in vigorous events, then, is what charms us in the novel of action. Why a mere description of violent actions should please us is a question for the psychologists; but there is no doubt that it does. In a novel of action a trifling event will have unexpected consequences; these will spread, and soon they will be numberless; an apparently inextricable web will be woven which will later be miraculously unravelled. In the action, its complication and its resolution, our interest is taken up; and being interested we are pleased. As the figures are roughly characterised, however, the events will evoke responses from them as well as serve to complicate the action. But the action is the main thing, the response of the characters to it incidental, and always such as to help on the plot. The actors have generally such characters, and so much character, as the action demands. In *Treasure Island* Trelawney must be unable to keep a secret, otherwise the pirates would never know he was sailing to find the treasure. Silver, in the same way, must be a diplomatist, otherwise the crew would not reach the island without being suspected; and the pirates must conveniently quarrel, or the few faithful hands would never win in the end. Had Silver and his followers killed all the loyal ship's company, secured the treasure, sailed away, been captured, taken to England and executed, *Treasure Island* would not have been a novel of action, but something else, probably of far greater value.

This novel which describes exceptional happenings in such a way as to please is probably the largest numerically of all classes of fiction. That class includes not only *Treasure Island*, but *Ivanhoe* and *The Cloister and the Hearth*, and on the other side a host of narratives of diminishing merit, ending in the popular tale of adventure or crime. All these stories imply by their nature a deviation from normal civilised life. *Ivanhoe* takes advantage of a civil insurrection, of a time when the normal forms of life were abrogated, of a historical period, too, when life was more dangerous; *Treasure Island* is a story of crime. The weightiness of its subject-matter, however, does not make the first any more important than the second; for what inspired the writer was the adventure itself, the escape from the uninteresting prosaic limitations of ordinary life. It is indispensable, then, that there should be an escape from life in the novel of action; but it is also indispensable that the escape should be perfectly safe. It must not only be thrilling, it must be temporary as well. The hero, having had his fling, must return to safety and order without a scar to prevent his enjoying them. Into the satisfying tumult he may be drawn by chance, or by love of danger; but he need be no more interested than the author in its significance. Consequently Scott's heroes are singularly incurious regarding the causes for which they are fighting; and so in *Old Mortality* he himself can remain admirably impartial as between the Prelatists and the Covenanters. Actually he is not much interested in them; the action, the unthinking escape, is the main thing.

In its course the novel of action will generally

deal out death to certain of the subsidiary characters; the wicked will be slaughtered, and some even of the good may safely be sacrificed, so long as the hero returns to peace and prosperity after his tumultuous vacation. The plot, in short, is in accordance with our wishes, not with our knowledge. It externalises with greater power than we ourselves possess our natural desire to live dangerously and yet be safe; to turn things upside down, transgress as many laws as possible, and yet escape the consequences. It is a fantasy of desire rather than a picture of life. It is never of much literary consequence except when, as in Scott and Stevenson, it is also in some measure a novel of character.

The novel of character is one of the most important divisions in prose fiction. Probably the purest example of it in English literature is *Vanity Fair*. *Vanity Fair* has no "hero"; no figure who exists to precipitate the action; no very salient plot; no definite action to which everything contributes; no end towards which all things move. The characters are not conceived as parts of the plot; on the contrary they exist independently, and the action is subservient

to them. Whereas in the novel of action particular events have specific consequences, here the
situations are typical or general, and designed
primarily to tell us more about the characters, or
to introduce new characters. As long as this is
done anything within probability may happen.
The author may invent his plot as he goes along,
as we know Thackeray did. Nor need the action
spring from an inner development, from a spiritual
change in the characters. It need not show us
any new quality in them, and at the time when it
is manifested. All it need do is to bring out
their various attributes, which were there at the
beginning; for these characters are almost always
static. They are like a familiar landscape, which
now and then surprises us when a particular effect
of light or shadow alters it, or we see it from a
new prospect. Amelia Sedley, George Osborne,
Becky Sharp, Rawdon Crawley—these do not
change as Eustacia Vye and Catherine Earnshaw
do; the alteration they undergo is less a temporal
one than an unfolding in a continuously widening
present. Their weaknesses, their vanities, their
foibles, they possess from the beginning and
never lose to the end; and what actually does

change is not these, but our knowledge of them.

The figures in *Vanity Fair* have this unchangeability, this completeness from the beginning; and this is one of the essential marks of the figures in the novel of character. We find those figures in Smollett, Fielding, and Sterne, in Scott, Dickens, and Trollope. Their unchangeability may seem at variance with truth, and it has often been called a fault. It is claimed that they should be more like "life"; that they should not keep one side always turned towards the reader; that they should revolve, showing us all their facets instead of an unchanging surface. Mr Forster calls those characters flat, and regrets that they should be flat. Yet they exist, and there must be some reason for their existence. In the novel of character they are to be met in thousands, and it is more reasonable to believe that there is method in their flatness than that they are mistakes which all the great character novelists have had the misfortune to commit. Why, indeed, should not a character be flat? The only real answer to this is that the present taste in criticism prefers round characters. The taste of the next generation may prefer flat, for all we know.   But the question is for what sufficient reason both kinds, the flat and the round, should exist.   Later in this essay I shall try to show that the flat character is the only one which could serve the purpose of the novelist of character, that it is his necessary vehicle for conveying one kind of vision of life.

Meanwhile, let us accept the unchangeability of flat characters as a quality rather than a fault. Given their flatness, what can the writer do with them?   What will the function of his plot be? Obviously not to trace their development, for being flat they cannot develop, but to set them in new situations, to change their relations to one another, and in all of these to make them behave typically.   The task of the character novelist is more like the choreographer's than the dramatist's; he has to keep his figures moving rather than acting; and for the most part he has them masked. So Becky Sharp must be introduced to Joe Sedley, to Sir Pitt Crawley, to the Marquis of Steyne, to Dobbin, to Lady Sheepshanks.   She must be "subjected" to them, combined with them, coloured by them; but at the same time she must show more clearly the characteristics we expect of her, or at any rate must always return to them.   The combinations will be as many as the novelist can invent, and if they are to have sufficient variety he must not be trammelled by a rigid plot, or by the need to develop his story dramatically.   He must have freedom to invent whatever he requires.   So it has been a convention that the plot of a novel of character should be loose and easy.   As in the novel of action the characters are designed to fit the plot; here the plot is improvised to elucidate the characters.   In *Treasure Island* the characters are general, the plot specific; in *Vanity Fair* the characters are specific, the situations general.

Thus far we have roughly distinguished two kinds of novel: one in which the plot must be strictly developed, and one in which it may best be loosely improvised.   These two types are, of course, easier to separate in theory than in practice; and in certain novels we find them confused.   It is difficult at first sight and formally to place such novels as *Roderick Random*, *Tom Jones*, *Old Mortality*, and *Martin Chuzzlewit*.   In all of them we shall find a great deal of action; one event leads on to another, and a happy solution of the entanglement is sought. We shall find, on the other hand, that the most successful characters are really independent of the main action, and that their responses are typical rather than useful. All these stories belong partly to the novel of action and partly to the novel of character; they strike a gentlemanly compromise, which the reader finds it worth his while to accept. There is all the machinery of make-believe—the appeal to curiosity, the reassuring end; but there is a considerable substratum of truth as well. *Roderick Random* and *Tom Jones* are picaresque novels; this is a very striking class in English fiction; it is unique in certain interesting particulars; and it may be considered separately.

The real aim of this form is obviously to provide a number of situations and a variety of objects for satirical, humorous, or critical delineation. In the eighteenth century the novel had not yet freed itself from the trammels of the story centred on a single figure who had always to be present, and though characterisation was then considered the main thing, the narrator remained on the centre of the stage. Perhaps he doubted the capacity of his characters to hold the reader's interest, and felt that an exciting story, containing adventures, was necessary. In any case a tale, centred on a hero, had to be kept going, and at the same time a number of characters had to be given an excuse for appearing. So we have the hard-worked travelling hero, posting from inn to inn, now in the country, now in London, knocking at the doors of the great, foregathering with rogues and thieves, languishing in prison or on board ship, suffering every vicissitude, good and bad; and enduring them all not because the novelist has any tender regard for his hero's sufferings or fortunes, but because he is avid of variety, and is determined to get a pass to as great a number of contrasting scenes as he can. This perhaps explains partly the cold-blooded manner in which Smollett puts his heroes through their paces, and his extreme insensitiveness to them. We see Roderick Random suffering agonies at school in Dumbartonshire; but we are not interested in his agonies, we have eyes only for the author's immensely effective portrait of the dominie who inflicts them. Roderick suffers again when he studies medicine; but we are only concerned with the quack who gulls him. On his road to London Roderick encounters all the oddities who could conceivably travel in a stage-coach, and not even the highwayman is left out. In London he is taught prudence by a pair of sharpers, and the arts of worldly advancement by a member of Parliament. But even this is not enough. The sea must be put under contribution, and Roderick enters the navy. By this time we cannot understand how he contrives to bear up under his sufferings; he has passed through enough to kill off three vigorous heroes; and we only make a sort of formal acknowledgment that he is still alive. All that happens to Roderick, then, could not possibly have happened to one man; but that was not of the slightest importance to Smollett, whose object was to give a picture of as many scenes and characters as possible, and in doing so to paint a broad picture of the life of his time.

The plot of *Tom Jones* is more probably and more closely constructed, but its object is the same. The central figure in *Roderick Random* is not very strictly characterised; he is obviously what he sets out to be, a piece of lively but necessary machinery. Tom Jones is a real character; he is the travelling hero, he is Fielding's

means of introducing a host of characters; but he
is as authentic as they.   Yet being a real character,
his actions had to be probable; he could not move
about with Roderick's lack of responsibility, nor
could such an astounding abundance of accidents
befall him.   He had, in short, to act the part of
a natural young man without an axe to grind,
while actually carrying on his business as a travelling tout for characters.   He does both; and
if as a consequence *Tom Jones* is less various
than *Roderick Random*, it is immensely superior
in continuous reality and verisimilitude.   Yet
brilliantly as it triumphs over the difficulties
inherent in the hero's double function, we always
feel those difficulties in the background.   The
plot of *Tom Jones* is an adroitly constructed
framework for a picture of life, rather than an
unfolding action.   The incidents are accurately
timed; they come in just where they should to
suit the scheme of the book; but they are never
inevitable; we do not see in them the logic of
action, but an exquisitely orderly mind arranging
everything for its own purpose.   This was, like
Smollett's, to take the reader on a panoramic tour
through society, a tour in which all the features

of interest would be unobtrusively indicated. From these two novels we may now draw, indeed, a further conclusion: that their object was not only to delineate character, but to give it in such variety as to suggest a picture of society. One of the aims of the novel of character is generally to do this; in this respect it stands apart from most other forms of the novel. Obviously Thackeray was interested in society, and as obviously Emily Brontë was very little interested in it.

The object of the picaresque novel is then to take a central figure through a succession of scenes, introduce a great number of characters, and thus build up a picture of society. There is an almost exact parallel to it in contemporary fiction: the recurring story of the young man who begins in poor circumstances and climbs vertically through all the social classes until he reaches the top. The counterpart of Smollett's travelling hero is Mr Wells's climbing hero. Travel was the chief means of becoming acquainted with the different manifestations of social life in the eighteenth century; success is the chief means to-day. Travel was difficult then; only a minority could

undertake it; and these were then in a position
to tell the majority how whole areas of society
lived with which it would never come into inti-
mate contact. Success is to-day as difficult as
communication was in the eighteenth century,
and it possesses the same advantages. The man
who has travelled or succeeded will, however, inevitably want to communicate his specially ac-
quired knowledge as well as to portray his characters; and in the picaresque novel, ancient and
modern, there is generally an attempt to provide
information such as a social student, or a moralist,
or an intelligent newspaper would give. This
is of some interest as corroborating by the wrong
means our theory that in the mind of the character
novelist there is generally, more or less promi-
nently displayed, a concern with the life of
society.

Old Mortality is a novel of a very different
kind. At first sight we might feel inclined to
put it among the novels of action and have done
with it. But it is a novel of character as well.
Apart from the main action, in a different world,
there are a few characters, Cuddie Headrigg and
his mother among them, who are not bound by

the plot, and act as independently as if they were in a different novel of their own. The hero, Henry Morton, is a typical novel-of-action figure. The story could quite well be carried forward by the chief roughly characterised figures, Morton, Claverhouse, Evandale, Burley. The real children of Scott's genius, here as in the other Waverley Novels, are supernumerary. These two sets of figures come into contact, but on a different plane from that on which the plot moves; and whenever they meet the surface movement of the story is suspended, and we get comedy which seems to make nonsense of the action, and suddenly exhibits it as make-believe. When we think of Scott's great characters, Cuddie Headrigg, Andrew Fairweather, Edie Ochiltree, Caleb Balderstone, we think of them as a chorus or as an audience to the artificially created action, the noise and fury, fundamentally uninteresting, which sink to the foreseen and insipid end. They help on the action by chance, or unwillingly, or with a sceptical detachment. Once, in Jeanie Deans, this type of character becomes the chief actor, and Scott writes the greatest of his novels. But mostly they are such as might appear in any picaresque novel, alongside Partridge, Parson Adams, or Lismahago, greater than they, but of the same family.

Scott was best, then, as a novelist of character. His heroes and heroines are wooden and unreal. The action has almost always an artificial origin. It does not arise from the passions of the hero, for the hero has generally a most gentlemanly incapacity for passion. It is never a necessary consequence of his disposition, for that, too, is mostly colourless. In these circumstances he can only be brought into action at all by being put into some arranged situation. He may, for instance; be caught up into a political struggle which he has not chosen, and in which he becomes involved by circumstances. His dangers are romantic, and quite apart from the "real world"; and he returns to mediocrity and himself very little changed by them. Once the action is set going, Scott's genius, it is true, makes it vigorous and real to a point; the roughly characterised men of action, Rob Roy, Claverhouse, Burley, speak as such figures might speak. They strike the resounding dramatic note; they have some of the passion and dignity appropriate to public figures; they are more vigorous than the historical recreations of any other novelist, than Dumas' Richelieu or Thackeray's Addison. Yet they never remain real for long, for there are other characters of more authentic reality to tell us so: Bailie Jarvie, Cuddie Headrigg, and all the rest. Scott's novels are the result of an unsatisfactory compromise. He is a fine novelist of action, and a great portrayer of character; and his right hand is always at war with his left. He is not so continuously delightful in narrative as Dumas, nor so perpetually rich in characterisation as Smollett. He was greater than either, but his vehicle of expression was so unsatisfactory that only by making allowances for it can we appreciate how rich his genius was.

The artificiality which marks Scott's novels becomes absurdly accentuated when we come to Dickens. The action in *Old Mortality* has a vigorous secondary reality; the action in Dickens' novels, except in a few late instances, is simple, melodramatic intrigue. In *Martin Chuzzlewit* we have one great creation, Pecksniff, and a host of delightful figures; but the action belongs to the cruder and more improbable kind of mystery story. The metamorphosis of Montague Tigg, the fascinating sponger, into an opulent company-promoter; his machinations against Jonas Chuzzlewit, ending in the murder; the deception practised by old Martin on Pecksniff for the purpose of unmasking him—compared with such things as these Scott's management of the action is serious and responsible. Dickens' plots, of course, were primarily intended to keep up the reader's interest from instalment to instalment of a serial. They had no literary function at all. To bring in his characters and set them going Dickens did not need such artifices; he had an exceptional talent in that direction. The meeting of old Martin Chuzzlewit's relatives in the beginning of the story, the visit of the Pecksniffs to Todgers', and with some reservations the journeyings of young Martin and Mark Tapley in the United States: these are brilliant strokes of comic invention, and Dickens is full of them. The plot in *Roderick Random* is a literary convention which fulfilled a purpose in its own time, though it is outmoded now. The plot in *Old Mortality* is quasi-real. But the plot of *Martin Chuzzlewit* has no reality at all; it is brought in to arouse interest which would have been keen in any case. Without it *Martin Chuzzlewit* would be infinitely better in every way.

It was Thackeray who first made a clear break with the plot both as a literary and a popular convention; and it was in this more clearly than in any other respect that he showed his superiority to Dickens in critical sense. Like the eighteenth-century novelists whom he admired so much, he set out to portray society; but if I am to do that, one might imagine him saying, why should I not do it directly? Why should I have an ambulating hero to take me from scene to scene? Why should I not *be* in any place where I want to be? So he starts with a number of characters drawn from various classes of social life. They meet in different places, move up or down the social scale, quarrel or agree, flatter or condescend, and as their lives unroll the complex of relationships and the number of characters expand until they embrace society. In *Vanity Fair* it is the progressive accumulation and rolling up of social relationships that creates the incidents and makes the plot. In naturalness, in consistence with itself, *Vanity Fair* is consequently superior to any English novel of character which preceded it.   The inessential and the inconsistent have been dropped.   There is as great a variety of figures as in *Tom Jones*; there is an equally comprehensive picture of life; but the picture unrolls of itself.   The plot of *Vanity Fair* has been compared adversely with that of *Tom Jones*.   We may admire the skilful conduct of Fielding's plot; yet after *Vanity Fair* no novelist of character could use such a convention again except for a different purpose—to write, perhaps, a fantastic or farcical story like *The Adventures of Harry Richmond*. For the serious portrayer of society it was outmoded.

In *Vanity Fair*, then, we start with the very society to which the plot of the picaresque novel was designed to introduce us.   All the plot that remains is the series of incidents which widen and diversify the picture, and set the characters in different relations.   These incidents may be quite trivial—a dinner, a theatre party, an unexpected meeting; or they may embrace some of the greater accidents of life—a love affair, a duel, a death.   What we ask from them is that they should arise as naturally as possible, that the plot should not appear to be a plot.

Next we must consider another form of the novel which, like the novel of action, demands a strictly developed plot.

II

THE DRAMATIC NOVEL

THIS is the dramatic novel. In this division the hiatus between the characters and the plot disappears. The characters are not part of the machinery of the plot; nor is the plot merely a rough framework round the characters. On the contrary, both are inseparably knit together. The given qualities of the characters determine the action, and the action in turn progressively changes the characters, and thus everything is borne forward to an end. At its greatest the affinity of the dramatic novel is with poetic tragedy, just as that of the novel of character is with comedy. The dialogue in the most intense scenes in *Wuthering Heights* and *Moby Dick* is hardly distinguishable from poetic utterance; the most memorable figures in *Vanity Fair* and *Tom Jones* are always on the verge of becoming purely comic figures like Falstaff or Sir Toby.

But in all its forms the dramatic novel need not be tragic, and the first novelist who practised it with consummate success in England—Jane Austen—consistently avoided and probably was quite incapable of sounding the tragic note. The instance may seem strange, but it is only so in appearance. The art of Jane Austen has a more essential resemblance to that of Hardy than to Fielding's or Thackeray's. There is in her novels, in the first place, a confinement to one circle, one complex of life, producing naturally an intensification of action; and this intensification is one of the essential attributes of the dramatic novel. In the second place, character is to her no longer a thing merely to delight in, as it was to Fielding, Smollett and Scott, and as it remained later to Dickens and Thackeray. It has consequences. It influences events; it creates difficulties and later, in different circumstances, dissolves them. When Elizabeth Bennett and Darcy meet first, the complexion of their next encounter is immediately determined. The action is set going by the changing tension between them and by a few acts of intervention on the part of the other figures; and the balance of all the forces within the novel creates and moulds the plot. There is no external framework, no merely mechanical plot; all is character, and all is at the same time action. One figure in the pure comedic sense there is in the book, Mr Collins. Mr Collins has no great effect on the action; he is an end, not a means and an end at the same time; he remains unchanged throughout the story. There are other pure comedic elements; for example, the permanent domestic tension between Mr and Mrs Bennett. But in most dramatic novels such figures and combinations are to be found. Hardy has his peasants to give relief and an additional emphasis of proportion to the action; they serve somewhat the same purpose as a sub-plot without being one. The real power of the Wessex Novels lies of course elsewhere, in the development of a changing tension making towards an end. If the chief power of *Pride and Prejudice* does not reside in that, at least half its power does.

The plot of *Pride and Prejudice* is very simple. "Why, my dear," says Mrs Bennett in the first chapter, "Mrs Long says that Netherfield is taken by a young man of large fortune from the north of

England." The mood of expectation is aroused; the young man arrives, and from that moment everything begins to move forward. Bingley is accompanied by his friend Darcy. There are visits and parties. Bingley—easy, good-natured, and impulsive—falls in love with Jane Bennett, and is ready to commit himself at once in spite of his distaste for her family; but his friend advises him against it and persuades him to leave the neighbourhood. Meanwhile Darcy discovers that he has fallen in love, against his judgment, with Jane's sister, Elizabeth; and after struggling against his inclination for a while, proposes in terms which she feels compelled to reject with some indignation. Certain things have happened meanwhile to create an aversion in her mind against Darcy. She has been repelled by his pride; she suspects that he has tried to alienate Bingley from her sister; and she has believed damaging stories about him. After the rejected proposal she receives a letter from Darcy which convinces her that she has been unjust. This is the crisis of the action, the Aristotelian middle of the plot. Everything thus far has moved towards it, but now everything moves towards a different end, determined by it. Darcy is seen to be the reverse of what Elizabeth had thought him; and the punctiliousness which before had made him appear absurd and disagreeable, now, in better circumstances, makes him pleasing. By his agency Bingley is restored to Jane, and Elizabeth, her feelings towards him describing the full circle, becomes his wife.

Where this plot differs from the plot of a novel of action is in its strict interior causation. The first aversion of Elizabeth for Darcy was inevitable because of the circumstances in which they met, because Darcy was proud of his social position and Elizabeth encumbered by her unpresentable family, and because they were people of such decided character that they were certain to dislike each other at the beginning. Elizabeth is true to the candour of her mind in believing Darcy to be cold, haughty and vindictive; she is equally true to it later in acknowledging that she is mistaken, and in changing her opinion. The action is created here by those characters who remain true to themselves; it is their constancy which, like a law of necessity, sets the events moving; and through these they gradually manifest themselves.

The correspondence in a novel of this kind between the action and the characters is so essential that one can hardly find terms to describe it without appearing to exaggerate; one might say that a change in the situation always involves a change in the characters, while every change, dramatic or psychological, external or internal, is either caused or given its form by something in both. In this respect the dramatic novel stands apart both from the novel of action and that of character. There is a hiatus between the plot and the characters in both; there should be none in the dramatic novel. Its plot is part of its significance.

But if in *Pride and Prejudice* a change in the situation involves a change in the characters, the propriety and truth of the progression, in other words of the plot, is of the first importance. That progression will be inevitable on two planes. It will have an inner truth in so far as it traces the unfolding of character, and an external truth inasmuch as it is a just development of the action. Or rather the identity of these two aspects of truth will here be complete, as it is in no other kind of novel. The novel of character, as I shall try to show later on, is concerned immediately only with the outside show of reality, and it implies beneath, not something corresponding to that, but something relatively incongruous with it. The novel of character brings out the contrast between appearance and reality, between people as they present themselves to society and as they are. The dramatic novel shows that both appearance and reality are the same, and that character is action, and action character.

Both these divisions of the novel may have equal æsthetic truth, then, but it is the identity with itself of the dramatic conception that gives its plot such organic and overpowering significance. Nothing in that plot is left out, or assumed. It may contain antithesis, but no mere contradictions. It will be logical in so far as the characters have something unchangeable in them which determines their responses to one another and to the situation. It will have a progression which is at once spontaneous and logical inasmuch as the characters will change, and the change will create new possibilities. This spontaneous and progressive logic is the real distinguishing feature of the plot of the dramatic novel. Everything does derive from factors stated and unalterable in the beginning; but at the same time the terms of the problem will alter, bringing about unforeseen results.

Both these elements, the logical and the spontaneous, necessity and freedom, are of equal importance in the dramatic plot. The lines of action must be laid down, but life must perpetually flood them, bend them, and produce the "erosions of contour" which Nietzsche praised. If the situation is worked out logically without any allowance for the free invention of life, the result will be mechanical, even if the characters are true. It is this logic without invention that makes Merimée's tales so curiously lifeless and negative in spite of their fine characterisation. His figures exist only in relation to the situation; they are equal to its requirements; they have no life beyond it. The immediate circumstance depresses a lever, and the action of the figures is prompt and absolutely complete. But these figures have no freedom to choose, to reflect, or even to postpone. Their will does not oppose, or even consider the action they are about to do; they are totally within it, like unreflecting animals. There is no dramatic tension in *Colomba* or *Carmen*; there is only action. The progression is logical, but it is not free; it has not the movement of life.

Some of Hardy's novels have the same fault in a much lesser degree. "The characters," Mr Forster remarks, "have to suspend their natures at every turn, or else are so swept away by the course of Fate that our sense of reality is weakened. . . . Hardy arranges events with emphasis on causality, the ground plan is a plot, and the characters are ordered to acquiesce in its requirements. His characters are involved in various snares, they are finally bound hand and foot, there is a ceaseless emphasis on fate, and yet, for all the sacrifices made to it, we never see the action as a living thing as we see it in *Antigone*, or *Berenice*, or *The Cherry Orchard*. The fate above us, not the fate working through us—that is what is eminent and memorable in the Wessex novels." "There is some vital problem," he says again, "that has not been answered, or even posed, in the misfortunes of *Jude the Obscure*. In other words, the characters have been required to

contribute too much to the plot; except in their
rustic humours, their vitality has been impover-
ished, they have gone dry and thin." No doubt
necessity is too obviously stressed in the Wessex
novels, and Hardy's reply to all questions is pre-
mature and far too sweeping. Certain vital prob-
lems are never posed; yet Mr Forster overstates
Hardy's defects. He overlooks the immense
power of invention which gives the Wessex novels
a living movement in spite of the encroachments
of the plot.

When freedom is overstressed the effect is
equally false. There is a notorious instance of
this in *Jane Eyre*, a novel which just misses being
truly dramatic. Jane loves Rochester, but she
will not live with him while his wife is alive; this
is the real dramatic problem. All Jane's character, all that should of necessity decide the
direction of the action, is summed up in her
refusal to go against her conscience. The story
should have been worked out to the end on this
assumption. Instead, Charlotte Brontë has the
insane Mrs Rochester conveniently burned to
death; she defeats fate, she defeats Jane, making
her qualities irrelevant and meaningless, by intro-

ducing an accident containing a very curious mixture of amiability, cruelty, and nonsense. Up to this point the story has been worked out dramatically; afterwards it is arranged by the author. In the plot of a dramatic novel a falsehood like this is a fundamental one, affecting the whole—action, characters, everything. In *The Newcomes* Thackeray, "by a most monstrous blunder . . . killed Lady Farintosh's mother at one page and brought her to life at another." We hardly notice it; we do not care much what becomes of the plot. But Charlotte Brontë could not make a single false move in the plot of *Jane Eyre* without giving a wrong direction to the whole book. She made a resounding one, and the result is calamitous.

Wuthering Heights is more totally impressive than either *Jane Eyre* or *The Return of the Native*, because the balance between necessity and freedom is held more tautly, and therefore more evenly, and proportion is won through the very intensity of the strain which these two forces impose on each other. How strictly the plot was worked out the reader may learn from a valuable little essay by an anonymous writer, published by

the Hogarth Press.[1]   Here it is shown that the
framework of necessity, legal and temporal, within
which the action was to take place, was carefully
worked out by the author.   To see after this how
spontaneous, how free from disfigurement by the
plot, the action is, he has only to turn to the book
itself.   All on the one side seems to be freedom,
all on the other is necessity.   Catherine and Heathcliff act of their own will, and their action is
perfect freedom; yet at the same time they are
figures in a tragedy whose terms and end are
ordained from the beginning.   The progression
in both dimensions is unerring, and it is one
progression.

To return to *Pride and Prejudice*, the foreknowledge of this progression can be very powerfully
felt in the account of Elizabeth's first meeting
with Darcy.   This is how Jane Austen describes
it:

Elizabeth Bennett had been obliged, by the scarcity
of gentlemen, to sit down for two dances; and during
part of that time, Mr Darcy had been standing near
enough for her to overhear a conversation between him

---

[1] *The Structure of Wuthering Heights*, by C. P. S. (The
Hogarth Essays).

and Mr Bingley, who came from the dance for a few minutes to press his friend to join it.

" Come, Darcy," said he, " I must have you dance. I hate to see you standing about by yourself in this stupid manner. You had much better dance." . . .

" You are dancing with the only handsome girl in the room," said Mr Darcy, looking at the eldest Miss Bennett.

" Oh! she is the most beautiful creature I ever beheld! But there is one of her sisters sitting down just behind you, who is very pretty, and I dare say very agreeable. Do let me ask my partner to introduce you."

" Which do you mean? " and turning round, he looked for a moment at Elizabeth, till catching her eye, he withdrew his own and coldly said, " She is tolerable, but not handsome enough to tempt me; and I am in no humour at present to give consequence to young ladies who are slighted by other men. You had better return to your partner and enjoy her smiles, for you are wasting your time with me."

Mr Bingley followed his advice. Mr Darcy walked off; and Elizabeth remained with no very cordial feelings towards him. She told the story, however, with great spirit among her friends; for she had a lively, playful disposition, which delighted in anything ridiculous.

This chance encounter starts the train of incidents which lead to Elizabeth's marriage to

Darcy, and as it is narrated we are made to feel a premonition of something like this. In its tentativeness, it informs us that it is a step merely, implying not merely a succession of scenes, but a development. If we compare it with a typical incident in *Vanity Fair*, we shall see the difference. The passage describes Becky Sharp's first meeting with Sir Pitt Crawley.

> The shutters of the first-floor windows of Sir Pitt's mansion were closed—those of the dining-room were partially open, and the blinds neatly covered up in old newspaper.
>
> John, the groom, who had driven the coach alone, did not care to descend to ring the bell; and so prayed a passing milk-boy to perform that office for him. When the bell was rung, a head appeared between the interstices of the dining-room shutters, and the door was opened by a man in drab breeches and gaiters, with a dirty old coat, a foul old neckcloth lashed round his bristly neck, a shining bald head, a leering red face, a pair of twinkling grey eyes, and a mouth perpetually on the grin.
>
> "This Sir Pitt Crawley's?" says John, from the box.
>
> "Ees," says the man at the door, with a nod.
>
> "Hand down these 'ere trunks, then," said John.
>
> "Hand'n down yourself," said the porter.

" Don't you see I can't leave my hosses? Come, bear a hand, my fine feller, and Miss will give you some beer," said John, with a horse-laugh, for he was no longer respectful to Miss Sharp, as her connection with the family was broken off, and she had given nothing to the servants on coming away.

The bald-headed man, taking his hands out of his breeches pockets, advanced on this summons, and throwing Miss Sharp's trunk over his shoulder, carried it into the house.

" Take this basket and shawl, if you please, and open the door," said Miss Sharp, and descended from the carriage in much indignation. " I shall write to Mr Sedley and inform him of your conduct," said she to the groom.

She was shown into the dining-room by the porter.

Two kitchen chairs, and a round table, and an attenuated old poker and tongs were gathered round the fireplace, as was a saucepan over a feeble sputtering fire. There was a bit of cheese and bread, and a tin candle-stick on the table, and a little black porter in a pint-pot.

" Had your dinner, I suppose? It is not too warm for you? Like a drop of beer? "

" Where is Sir Pitt Crawley? " said Miss Sharp majestically.

" He, he! *I'm* Sir Pitt Crawley. Reklect you owe me a pint for bringing down your luggage. He, he! Ask Tinker if I aynt. Mrs Tinker, Miss Sharp: Miss Governess, Mrs Charwoman. Ho, ho! "

These two passages are fairly typical of Jane Austen and Thackeray, and the difference between them is salient. It is that Jane Austen's scene can only be completed by other scenes to which it is leading up; while Thackeray's is in a sense complete in itself. We know the characters in it immediately and altogether, because at the start they behave typically, as their generalised selves, and there is nothing for them but to keep on doing so. We will not know Elizabeth and Darcy, however, until the action has revealed them to us. The scene from *Pride and Prejudice* is not merely one which may, but one which must be followed by others. These, moreover, must be unlike it, rather than of the same quality: a differentiation of the particular, not a repetition of the typical, as the scenes in the novel of character are.

This being so, however, those scenes postulate an end. The reader is gradually led to a consciousness of this end; but to the writer it is known from the beginning, and it is a vague apprehension of this, perhaps, not consciously recognised by us, that gives to the action of a story like *Wuthering Heights* that enigmatic significance

which we can never analyse. When Emily
Brontë is describing an intermediate scene, the
whole compass of her characters' lives, all that
they have been, all that the future has in store
for them, is involuntarily implied in it. Her plot
must have been in her mind as a complete pattern
from the beginning, and the characters must have
existed there, not in their diurnal, invariable
form, but in movement, in their entire changing
transit through time. Thackeray's characters,
on the other hand, being perpetually complete
and perpetually the same, might well have been
herded loosely in his mind; there is no tension
within them or in the action into which he puts
them. There is this tension in dramatic characters;
the tension between their completeness seen as
fate, and their progression seen as development.
In the very conception of them there is the
problem of time. Time surrounds Becky Sharp,
it is true; but it reveals Catherine Earnshaw.
It is the element in which she unfolds and
in which finally her fate is consummated. The
end in the dramatic novel is therefore of extraordinary significance; not merely a rounding
off of the story as in *Vanity Fair*, but the final

illumination.   It is the end not only of the action, but of the characterisation; the last touch which gives finality and completeness to the revelation of the figures. The people of the character novelist, as they live in a state of perpetual completeness, are not in need of this final touch.   His plot need not be complete from the beginning, simply because his characters are complete at the beginning.

The end of any dramatic novel will be a solution of the problem which sets the events moving; the particular action will have completed itself, bringing about an equilibrium, or issuing in some catastrophe which cannot be pursued farther. Equilibrium or death, these are the two ends towards which the dramatic novel moves. The first, for various reasons, generally takes the form of a suitable marriage.

So much at present for the temporal progression and the end of the dramatic novel. Coming back to *Pride and Prejudice* we may take up now the other respect in which it diverges from the character novel; its confinement to a narrow scene, and to one complex of life. We shall find this concentration of the area of action in almost all dramatic novels. We find it in Hardy, in Emily Brontë, in *The House with the Green Shutters*, even in *Moby Dick*, where though the stage is vast, it is in a sense unchanged: there is no escape from it. The reason for the isolation of the scene in the dramatic novel is obvious enough. Only in a completely shut-in arena can the conflicts which it portrays arise, develop, and end inevitably. All the exits are closed, and as we watch the action we know this. There is no escape into other scenes, or if there is we know that they are false exits bringing the protagonist back to the main stage again, where he must await his destiny. The scene here is the framework within which the logic of the action can develop unimpeded, and shut off from the arbitrary interference of the external world. It gives necessity to that logic by defining the limits within which it may work.

Our conclusions may now be summed up generally before we proceed to amplify them. The plot of the character novel is expansive, the plot of the dramatic novel intensive. The action of the first begins with a single figure, as in *Roderick Random*, or with a nucleus, as in *Vanity Fair*, and expands towards an ideal circumference, which is an image of society. The action of the second, on the contrary, begins never with a single figure, but with two or more; it starts from several points on its circumference, which is a complex, not a nucleus, of personal relationships, and works towards the centre, towards one action in which all the subsidiary actions are gathered up and resolved. The novel of character takes its figures, which never change very much, through changing scenes, through the various modes of existence in society. The dramatic novel, while not altering its setting, shows us the complete human range of experience in the actors themselves. There the characters are changeless, and the scene changing. Here the scene is changeless, and the characters change by their interaction on one another. The dramatic novel is an image of modes of experience, the character novel a picture of modes of existence.

Starting from those general conclusions, we may now tentatively approach another. Keeping our eyes on those two divisions of the novel as they are, we must needs believe that neither could give us its characteristic sense of human variety if it did not observe its limitations.   Without its shut-in arena the one could not evoke such a range and absoluteness of experience in its figures.   Without the unchangeability of its types the other could not show us such a clear-cut diversity of character and manners.   It is here the static definition, the completeness of every character at every moment, that points the diversity and makes it self-evident. To see sharply the difference between a multitude of living things we must arrest their movement. They must not change while we look, or the change will confuse our sense of distinction; difference will merge at times into identity, to disentangle itself and to merge again.   By the same analogy, to produce a sense of diversity of character with the maximum effect, the figures must be rendered static, or rather must be seen as static, as certain types of imagination in fact see them.   If all this is so, however, the limitations of the dramatic and the character novel, in appearance arbitrary, are in reality reasonable and necessary, for only by observing them can the writer get his effect and externalise his peculiar vision of life.

III

TIME AND SPACE

Up till now I have had to simplify everything. I have spoken as if the divisions of prose fiction were pure categories; as if any example of the character or the dramatic novel were absolute and unmixed. There are of course no novels purely of character or merely of conflict; there are only novels which are predominantly the one or the other. This predominance, however, is always salient and always sufficient. The principle of *Wuthering Heights* is dramatic, though it contains a few characters, like old Joseph and Mrs Dean; the principle of *Vanity Fair* is not dramatic, though it contains several highly dramatic scenes, such as Rawdon Crawley's quarrel with the Marquis of Steyne. Nobody is likely to dispute this distinction, or to insist that it is absolute; and trusting to this, I can now go on to my next generalisation, which is that the imaginative world of the dramatic novel is in Time, the imaginative world of the character novel in Space.   In the one, this roughly is the argument, Space is more or less given, and the action is built up in Time;   in the other, Time is assumed, and the action is a static pattern, continuously redistributed and reshuffled, in Space.   It is the fixity and the circumference of the character plot that gives the parts their proportion and meaning;   in the dramatic novel it is the progression and resolution of the action.   The values of the character novel are social, in other words;   the values of the dramatic novel individual or universal, as we choose to regard them.   On the one hand we see characters living in a society, on the other figures moving from a beginning to an end.   These two types of the novel are neither opposites, then, nor in any important sense complements of each other;   they are rather two distinct modes of seeing life: in Time, personally, and in Space, socially.

As stated, this thesis may seem full of difficulties. How can a story have a spatial construction, seeing that in it certain things must happen, and some time, however short, must be consumed?

How can time be subordinate in any sense, seeing that every novel necessarily records the passing of time? But to say that a plot is spatial does not deny a temporal movement to it, any more, indeed, than to say that a plot is temporal means that it has no setting in space. Here, once more, it is all a question of the predominating element. The main object of the one plot is to proceed by widening strokes, and to agree that it does so is to imply space as its dimension. The main object of the other is to trace a development, and a development equally implies time. The construction of both plots will be inevitably determined by their aim. In the one we shall find a loosely woven pattern, in the other the logic of causality.

A more vivid sense of the meaning of this distinction can be evoked by calling to mind the different feeling of time and space in various novels. In the dramatic novel in general the articulation of space is vague and arbitrary. London might be a thousand miles away from Wuthering Heights or Casterbridge. But from the London of *Vanity Fair* and *Tom Jones*, on the other hand, every place has its just geographical distance, and no part of England, no small town, no country estate or remote parsonage is inaccessible; the gentry, the tradesmen, the peasantry, the post-boys, the innkeepers—the classes, rich and poor, are there, or at least some hypothetical provision is made for them. *Wuthering Heights* and *The Return of the Native*, on the contrary, blot out all that portion of England which lies beyond the concentrated scene of their action; the world outside is ghostly and remote, and the countless figures peopling it are quite forgotten, wiped out, as if the intensity and swiftness with which time consumes itself in the action had wasted them too. We are conscious of England in *Tom Jones* and *Vanity Fair*; we are only aware of the Yorkshire moors and Egdon Heath in *Wuthering Heights* and *The Return of the Native*.

Or consider another difference. By what seems at first a paradox we shall find in the dramatic novel a far more intense visual realisation of the scene than in the novel of character. No doubt this is partly because the scene in the former becomes coloured and dyed by the passions of the chief figures, because we always see them against it, and closed in by it.   But it is more essentially because the scene here—the scene in Hardy's novels and in *Wuthering Heights*—is not an ordinary and particular scene at all, like the Sedley's drawing-room, or Sir Pitt Crawley's country estate, but rather an image of humanity's temporal environment.   The Yorkshire moors and Wessex are not places differentiated and recognisable like Mr Bennett's Five Towns or Trollope's Barchester; they are universal scenes where the drama of mankind is played out.   As this drama, seen thus, is independent of temporal fashions, as the period with its manners, costumes, and habits, and all the other properties of changing civilisation, are in a sense irrelevant to it, the scene will be primitive: Egdon Heath, or "the harebells and limestone" of Emily Brontë's Yorkshire moors, or the oceans over which Ahab pursues the White Whale.   When we think of Thackeray's characters we think of them in the costume and against the background of their time; their clothes, the houses they live in, and the fashions they observe, are part of their reality; they exist in their period as in a suddenly fixed world.   But we recall Hardy's figures as we recall things which are amenable to no fashions save those of nature; as we remember heaths, rocks, and trees. The scene against which he sets his men and women has not essentially changed since the time when figures capable of the few universal emotions with which he endows them might have lived in it. Space here, then, is undifferentiated and universal, though apparently narrow, an image of the world itself, and moreover unchangeable, for no matter what fashions may alter the surface of human life, in this way, a mind like Hardy's will always be able to see the world. The scene here, in short, is the earth, as in the novel of character it is civilisation. The power which Hardy's landscapes exercise is drawn from nature directly, and his characters are bound by as strong ties to the earth as to each other.

But those natural potencies which have such influence over Hardy's characters will be little felt in Thackeray's scenes, which are cut off from nature, as by a wall, by the observances of society. To the social parlours of Barchester, to the prosperous middle-class villas of the Five Towns, they will reach with difficulty. But, on the other hand, we will be shown by the character novelist that the human scene, that world in itself, is infinitely various and interesting; that Queen's Crawley is a very different place from Russell Square, and that there is an inexhaustible diversity of places and states of life in the Five Towns. We shall see the universal becoming particularised; humanity in all its varieties of prison-house, ornamental or plain; and if we are no longer conscious of the earth, we become free citizens of society, with a pass to all sorts of places.

Or take another striking difference, between the feeling of time in the character and the dramatic novel; how it seems to linger in the one and fly in the other. If we open *Vanity Fair* at the first chapter and listen to Becky Sharp, and then take it up towards the end, when we know that a great number of things have happened and many years elapsed, we shall have a curious feeling of having marked time, of still being on the same spot; somewhat the same feeling one might have if one were to fall asleep in a room where people were discussing some question, and wake up to find the discussion at exactly the same stage. In the last chapters of *Vanity Fair* Becky is still talking very much as she did in the first. Let us turn

next to the passage which introduces Catherine
Earnshaw, and to her last interview with Heathcliff. There the shock we receive is of a different
kind. We know at once that while we have been
sleeping something extraordinary has happened;
Time, almost like a physical process, has passed
over the figure of Catherine. This test may be
applied to any great dramatically conceived figure
except for a few like Captain Ahab in *Moby Dick*.
For Ahab does not change; the action of the whole
book, indeed, hardly moves for a while; there is
only the long stretch of description, reverie, waiting, and then the fatal combat described in the
last few chapters; a combat which we do not see
approaching, which could only come suddenly,
absent one moment, unconditionally present the
next; neither to be courted in its absence, nor
when it is there avoided. With its static characters and sudden calamitous movement, *Moby
Dick* occupies a place somewhat apart from the
ordinary dramatic novel. But it is an exception
which throws light on the point we are considering. In *Moby Dick* Melville was not dealing with
the ordinary world where good and evil are mixed,
where passion is both noble and sordid, and there

is right on both sides, as there is in *Wuthering Heights*. He was portraying a world purged as nearly as possible of the intermediate and the mixed; and on the most inhuman of arenas, the sea, he set two absolute forces against each other, the symbolical figures of Ahab and the White Whale. The enmity between these two is not human; it is not a thing which could arise through some accident of Time, and develop and suffer enhancement or diminution, like everything of this world; it is there from the beginning, not a feeling which must be fed if it is to grow, but a force which cannot be altered. The drama in *Moby Dick* is, then, a drama of opposites, and as neither can yield, the conflict had to be simple, catastrophic, and without a development. There is a very strong sense of time in the book, it is true, but not the sense of time which we find in Hardy or Emily Brontë. For an age the action stands still, with an almost intolerable vacancy of expectation and deferred crisis, as if the ship's company were foundering in a stagnant sea of Time; then in the last few chapters all seems to burn away in a breath-space.

As this urgency of time in the dramatic novel

is one of its essential characteristics, we must consider it a little further. The scenes in a dramatic novel postulate an end, as we have seen, and in the greatest we have a sense that the end is known. In other words, we have a prescience of something *definite* to come; and it is this alone that articulates and vivifies future time for us, so that it no longer seems a mere impersonal process, or a vacant succession, but becomes a presence, hostile or auspicious, capable of destroying our peace, or of bringing us happiness. In a story like *The Return of the Native*, first we have a vague apprehension of the end towards which things are moving. Eustacia Vye's ambition and passion will lead her to some exceptional destiny, brilliant or calamitous; but everything is undetermined as yet. With the arrival of Clym Yeobright her destiny begins to take shape; for a moment it seems to be leading her to happiness; then Clym's blindness and fanaticism alter everything. As yet the end is in the distance; but time has begun to accelerate, and only something extraordinary can slow it down. There follows the scene where Mrs Yeobright walks over the heath to visit Eustacia, and turned away while Clym is sleeping, dies on her way back. This is the turning point in the story; the end is brought close to Eustacia, and after her last interview with Clym there is nothing between her and the moment towards which all her life she has been moving. Up to the last phase only the creator of Eustacia has known this moment and when it would come, but now we know it too. And in this brief interval between our knowledge of the end and its coming all Eustacia's transit through life is realised as if for the first time, and in our realisation has been ended.

In the beginning of a dramatic novel such as this, then, we see Time gradually gathering itself up; then beginning to move, its end still unknown to us; then as its goal becomes clearer, marching with a steady acceleration; and finally fate is there and all is finished. This end may coincide with the end of the book, as in *Tess of the D'Urbervilles*, or it may come before, leaving a pause, as in *The Mayor of Casterbridge*, or it may be the main crisis, as in *Wuthering Heights*, where Heathcliff is no longer completely there after the last interview with Catherine in the middle of the book; the drama is over, and only his suffering remains.

No one, perhaps, has understood better than Dostoevsky this naked manifestation of Time at the moment when it is slipping away; and a passage in *The Idiot* describing the feelings of a man condemned to death explains it with great force, and gives at the same time the reason why those scenes in the dramatic novel should have such extraordinary power. Prince Muishkin is describing an execution he had seen at Lyons. "Well, at all events," someone says, "it is a good thing that there's no pain when the poor fellow's head flies off."

"Do you know, though," the Prince replies, "you made that remark now, and everyone says the same thing, and the machine is designed with the purpose of avoiding pain, this guillotine, I mean; but a thought came into my head then: What if it should be a bad plan after all? You may laugh at my idea, perhaps—but I could not help its occurring to me all the same. Now with the rack and tortures and so on—you suffer terrible pain of course; but then your torture is bodily pain only (although no doubt you have plenty of that) until you die. But here I should imagine the most terrible part of the whole punishment is, not the bodily pain at all—but the certain knowledge that in an hour—then in ten minutes, then in half a minute, then now—this very *instant*—your soul must quit your body and that you will no longer be a man—and that this is certain, *certain!* That's the point—the certainty of it. Just that instant when you place your head on the block and hear the iron grate over your head—then—that quarter of a second is the most awful of all."

Here Dostoevsky shows in what ways the knowledge of something to come can change and at the same time bring out the values of time. In the instance he describes the knowledge is certainty, and the thing to come is death. The end of a dramatic novel is very seldom known with certainty, however, either to the actors or to the reader. The effect of the acceleration of time in it is therefore at once less painful and more complex than here. No doubt the author's foreknowledge contributes something to that effect; seeing what is to come he will communicate his forebodings of the event before it is revealed;

and his utterance will warn us, while the protagonists are still unconscious of their fate.

Or the characters may for long foresee their fate as an incredible possibility; fearing it and yet not crediting their fears. It is the expectation of this event dreaded and yet inconceivable that gives *The Idiot* its painful tension, and makes the conclusion so powerful, at once an exposure and a fulfilment of the whole action. Again and again throughout the book there are hints prefiguring the end, which, as everyone knows, is the murder of Nastasia by Rogojin; there are perhaps too many of these, indeed, and in places the symbolism becomes clever and obvious. But in the scene where Prince Muishkin returns from Moscow and goes to see Rogojin at his Petersburg house, there is an admirable foreshadowing incident. Only a third of the story has been told, but the end is already throwing wild shadows over the action.

Muishkin and Rogojin have been talking of various things.

"Let go of it!" said Parfen, seizing from the prince's hand a knife which the latter had at that moment taken up from the table, where it lay beside the history book. Parfen replaced it where it had been.

" I seemed to know it—I felt it, when I was coming back to Petersburg," continued the prince. " I did not want to come, I wished to forget all this, to uproot it from my memory altogether! Well, good-bye— what is the matter? "

He had absently taken up the knife a second time, and again Rogojin snatched it from his hand, and threw it down on the table. It was a plain looking knife, with a bone handle, a blade about eight inches long, and broad in proportion; it did not clasp.

Seeing that the prince was considerably struck by the fact that he had twice seized this knife out of his hand, Rogojin caught it up with some irritation, put it inside the book, and threw the latter across to another table.

" Do you cut your pages with it or what? " asked Muishkin, still rather absently, as though unable to throw off a deep preoccupation into which the conversation had thrown him.

" Yes."

" It's a garden knife, isn't it? "

" Yes. Can't you cut pages with a garden knife? "

" It's quite new."

" Well, what of that? Can't I buy a new knife if I like?" shouted Rogojin furiously, his irritation growing with every word.

The prince shuddered, and gazed fixedly at Parfen. Suddenly he burst out laughing.

" Why, what an idea! " he said. " I didn't mean to ask you any of these questions; I was thinking of something quite different! But my head is heavy, and I seem so absent-minded nowadays! Well, good-bye—I can't remember what I wanted to say—good-bye! "

There the vague suspicion that Rogojin will try to murder him is accompanied in the prince's mind by the shadowy prescience of some act farther away which he cannot catch; it is the premonition that this knife will be used to kill Nastasia. This shadow of knowledge in his mind is like something he has dreamt of and dismissed without being able to unriddle it. The whole passage is masterly. Dostoevsky's intention seems to be to suggest so often and so openly that Rogojin will end by murdering Nastasia that it becomes the one thing that nobody expects because everybody says it. One such scene as this would have prepared us for the murder; but Dostoevsky gives us scene after scene until a mood almost of security is built up. Yet at the same time, more and more unbelievable the oftener it is mentioned, the fear remains; and it is from this double tension of incredulity and fear, too painful almost, that the murder at last gives us relief. One or two of the characters actually experience in advance those moments of fascinated terror which come from foreknowledge of murder; but then those moments become part of their memory of the past, and therefore no longer to be dreaded; and so they continue to say in security, as if it were an old story, that Rogojin will murder Nastasia. The end, which comes suddenly and unexpectedly, lights up everything which led up to it; fate which had been playing hide-and-seek for so long manifests itself, and shows the action in one instant as it is. Into this instant all the time traversed by the action seems to fly, transformed and ended by the same stroke.

In *The Idiot* the sense of the urgency of time is given by a particular fear, by the knowledge, sometimes hidden, but always revealed again, of a definite event that will happen. In *Wuthering Heights* it is given by a fear more vast and shadowy; by the apprehension of something terrible, but unknown. In *The Idiot* the characters and the reader foresee the definite act of violence which lies in wait; the action consequently awakens a painful emotion somewhat similar to that of the condemned man whose story Dostoevsky, with marvellous art, introduces in the first few pages. But in *Wuthering Heights* the end is foreseen by a consciousness neither ours nor that of Heathcliff or Catherine. In so far as it is foreseen it is definite; but to us it is not yet in the realm of Time; it is rather something which at a pre-destined moment will appear in Time, when it will be as palpable as the last action in *The Idiot*, and as luminously as that will light up the action, during its progress dark and only in part manifest. We know that Heathcliff's and Catherine's love will end in disaster; yet that disaster has no recognisable shape for us, and is limited by no one significance. Until it falls it is an image of every potentiality of disaster, and we are given a sense of possibility, of freedom, which is absent in Dostoevsky's novel. In *Wuthering Heights* Heathcliff and Catherine seem to be freely choosing their fate without knowing it; in *The Idiot* Rogojin, Muishkin, and Nastasia are driven helplessly towards a fate they foresee and cannot escape. The sense of Time in the two novels is accordingly very dissimilar; in *The*

Idiot the characters wander in a daze, living in that nightmare state, known sometimes in our dreams, in which there are innumerable things which we must do, but we cannot remember them, or we do not know which to do first. Almost from beginning to end Muishkin, Rogojin, and Nastasia are fighting against time, and it is this that gives the book its hurried and urgent movement. In *Wuthering Heights*, on the other hand, Catherine and Heathcliff, unconscious of their fate, fly towards it with a single unhesitating flight. Time passes in both novels swiftly, but in the one with a rush of freedom, in the other with an unwilling haste.

The feeling of time may be vastly dissimilar in different dramatic novels, then; our apprehension of the end towards which it is moving may be definite or indefinite; the march of the action may be slower or faster; but enough, perhaps, has been said to show that the sense of time running out gives the real edge to the dramatic emotion.

In the dramatic novel, then, as in all dramatic literature, time moves and will therefore move to its end and be consumed. In the novel of character at its best we feel that time is inexhaustible. The great character creations, Uncle Toby, Parson Adams, Lismahago, Mr Collins, Cuddie Headrigg, Micawber, are beyond time and change, just as the great dramatic figures are completely enclosed in them and subject to them. In no novel of character, of course, is time quite stationary, though certain of the characters may remain so; but the more time is slowed down or ignored—the more all urgency is taken from it— the more favourable does it become for the emergence of characters. There is something humorous, something giving a sense of security, in the very slowing down of time, as may be seen in *Tristram Shandy*, *Ulysses*, and the slow-motion picture. Marvell's often-quoted poem, "To his Coy Mistress," is an admirable illustration of this. Thinking how he would woo "Had we but world enough, and time," he uses images which involuntarily become humorous:

> I would
> Love you ten years before the Flood,
> And you should, if you please, refuse
> Till the conversion of the Jews.

Then comes the turning-point in the poem, and all becomes urgent and dramatic:

> But at my back I always hear
> Time's winged chariot hurrying near . . .
> Now let us sport us as we may;
> And now like amorous birds of prey
> Rather at once our Time devour
> Than languish in his slow-chapped power . . .
> Thus, though we cannot make our Sun
> Stand still, yet we will make him run.

If one wanted an image of the world of character one might without extravagance see it in the first part of this poem, just as one might see the world of dramatic action in the second.

We must not separate these worlds too rigidly, however. In all dramatic novels we shall find visitors from the world of character; in all character novels dramatic scenes. Hardy's peasants, Emily Brontë's old Joseph, change as little as Uncle Toby or Andrew Fairweather. But they do not hold the stage like these. They exist in a secondary world; they inhabit a sort of stationary dream. They look out; they see the altering scene around them; and this scene is the dramatic action, which to them, in the same

way, has the appearance of a swiftly changing
dream. For this reason Falstaff, as we recreate
him in our imagination, remains quite unthreatened by the violent events in the two parts
of *Henry IV*; the world in which Prince Henry
and Hotspur fight and the king dies is not his
world, but only a dream which passes over it.
Time is the central reality in that dream, and
Time passes him by.

It is this imperviousness to time, this almost
mythical permanence, which deepens our delight
in such figures as Falstaff, Uncle Toby, Cuddie
Headrigg, and Mr Micawber. To admit that
they were capable of change would be to limit
their significance, not to enrich it; changed, they
would no longer be universal in their place, which
is a stationary spatial world in which time has
reached an equilibrium. This is the reason why,
when Dickens fits out Micawber with a new
existence at the end of *David Copperfield*, the
effect is so displeasing. Not only is a term set to
a delight which seemed unending, but Micawber
himself is at one stroke robbed of his eternal
validity. We still think of him as everlastingly
"waiting for something to turn up," it is true,

for our imagination ignores the last transformation, and gives him back to us as he was. Yet Dickens' mistake harms Micawber, as Shakespeare's, marvellous as it is, harms Falstaff. Our imagination gives us back Falstaff, too, as he lived, in spite of the pathos of the death scene. His death is less a part of his life than a term set to it; and the shadow that mortality casts back upon him is so imperceptible that he seems as unthreatened by it as Uncle Toby, or Mr Collins, who do not die at all. We know that like these he will always exist, and always be the same.

This, then, is the mark of all the principal creations of the character novelist; it is of their life, and of that alone, that we are aware, not of their life and death, not of that double fate which colours all dramatic figures. The true character seems to exist equally in all time, and untouched by time. *Vanity Fair* is no more a picture of Victorian society than of society itself; it does not show us only how people lived in Victoria's reign, but how people live in civilised society. It can justly, therefore, be called a picture of life or of manners; but the definition does not apply to the other divisions of the novel. The dramatic novel is rather a development reproducing the organic movement of life; and if we may take up an analogy without following it too far, is more like a movement in a symphony than a picture.

So much for the temporal vacancy of the novel of character; its spatial vitality, if this analysis should be accepted by anyone, will appear as obvious. There is in the great character novels a feeling of intensely filled space as extraordinary in its way as the feeling of crowded time in the dramatic novel. The almost nightmare luxuriance of life in Dickens' London; the mob of characters who jostle one another in his books, so that the scene seems crammed to bursting-point: this intensity of spatial reality, which can only be found in the character novel, is the counterpart of the intensity of time in the chief scenes in *Wuthering Heights* and the conclusion of *Moby Dick*. When we think of the world of characters, the picture that comes before us is something like those crowded frontispieces which used to adorn the collected editions of Dickens' novels, where we see standing side by side, and one behind the other, the forms of Mr Pickwick,

Pecksniff, Micawber, Dick Swiveller, Uriah Heep, Sam Weller, Sairey Gamp, Montague Tigg, The Artful Dodger, The Fat Boy, and a host of minor figures, until the page seems to be unable to hold any more. This crowded effect, this sense of living and moving space, is produced, once more, by the unchangeability of the characters. None of them ceases to occupy his place when another appears; all existing permanently, all exist contemporaneously; and even if they have their places in separate novels, we think of them together. It is as if the talent of the character novelist could only propagate itself by fission, where the dramatic genius observes the narrower limitations of reproduction; the variety of the first remaining purely spatial, where that of the other, being organic, can only be manifested in time. We think of Dickens' and Thackeray's characters as all living at the same time, and as all living forever, and we think of them, therefore, as a crowd. But Emily Brontë's figures appear to us singly; Space may from out its distances throw them together, but one by one they disappear from it, and at last they leave it vacant.

Why should those two forms of the novel be bound by the limitations which we have been discussing? Why should not the action develop with equal freedom in Time and in Space? This is the question which we must consider next.

IV

THE CHRONICLE

THE dramatic novel is limited in Space and free in Time, the character novel limited in Time and free in Space; why should this be so? The question was answered partially in an earlier chapter. It was the closed-in arena, we held, that gave the dramatic conflict intensity, and accelerated and emphasised the passage of time. It was the unchangeability of the characters, on the other hand, that made typical those relations between them which imaged the life of society. These reasons are perhaps sufficient in themselves to justify the formal limitations of those two divisions. The resources of prose narrative being what they are, they could hardly be employed with more economy and effect than here. But to understand fully the æsthetic virtues of those two methods of representation, we must try to find other reasons for them than simple necessity.

It is a commonplace that there are two elements in a work of art: a universal and a particular. The artist sets out to describe the particular and that alone; the universal is not directly and immediately conveyed; it has been brought to birth with the particular, but how we do not know. What do we mean, however, by the universal? Certain arts seem to have a validity only in one dimension, as sculpture and painting in space, and music in time. Plastic art becomes "literary" and loses some of its characteristic force when it tries to convey the realities of time; music, in the same way, loses something when it deviates from its pure temporal movement. Both these arts are more unmixed than the art of imaginative literature, and very much more so than the novel, which is the most complex and formless of all its divisions. But prose fiction is an art, and an art only by virtue of its possessing universality; and the universalising laws governing other forms must govern it too. The operation of those laws may not be so immediately perceptible in the novel, but their authority is final.

An idea of what we mean by universality can, curiously enough, be most easily given in negatives.

Seen negatively, the absolute validity of a statue seems to consist in the fact that it is independent of time, that of a piece of music in the fact that it is beyond space. But this apparent absence is in reality not mere absence, but something else. To banish time or space is not a negative action, but a difficult achievement; it is not done by omitting something which everybody normally does, but by accomplishing an unusual act of concentration. The annihilation of time in the statue and of space in music has in reality the effect of making both absolute. The plastic artist, concentrated on his spatial image and on that alone, attains a state which we justifiably call timeless; the processes of time have stopped for him, or have become irrelevant. The same with the musician, building up a movement in time, until the barriers of space disappear and he exists in infinity. This act of annihilation or universalisation—however we may name it— is only achieved by the unconditionality of the artist's concentration on something else, the particular object; it is an indirect conquest, the infinite shadow of his particular and definite accomplishment.

Let us follow the painter and the musician a little farther before we return to the novel with its less clear-cut and absolute laws. What gives the painter his particulars for a picture is the world of space: trees, rocks, houses, people, landscapes, lights, shadows, anything that the eye can see. What makes his vision of those things absolute is the moment of supreme concentration in which time is annihilated, and in that annihilation is made unconditional. It is as if in ignoring time, he renders it present untouched, unparticularised, and therefore universal. If he had made the universal his subject-matter, and essayed it directly, he would only have been able to achieve a parable concerning it; for it cannot be stated concretely; it can only be there when the particular is evoked. The background of eternity or of infinity, then, or of something suggesting one of these, is necessary to give the particular form, whether plastic or musical, its universality, and make it absolute.

This, of course, does not mean that the universality of a picture consists in its obliviousness of time, or the universality of a piece of music in its forgetfulness of space. These are elements merely, or rather symptoms. Once it is achieved, universality is simply universality. In a great work of art all seems particular, and at the same time all seems universal. Attained, the universal puts its stamp on all the parts, permeates the whole form or the complete movement.

Let us now return to the novel. I took the instances of painting and music, not only because their laws were more clear-cut than the laws of the novel, but because I had already drawn a rough analogy between painting and the novel of character, and music and the dramatic novel. Picking up those divisions again, we see now that their limitations are really essential to them as works of art, as works possessing universality. The unimportance or the unreality of time is neither a fault in the character novel nor an arbitrary attribute of it, but the condition which alone sets its pictures of life beyond the influence of change. The undifferentiated spatial setting is, again, not an accidental limitation of the dramatic novel, but the element which makes its movement a movement in infinity. The boundaries which confine those two types of the novel are in reality the condition of their universality.

This, then, will be our justification for the limitations of those two forms. It may be still further strengthened, perhaps, by a psychological fact which many people must have noted. We actually understand life more fully when we see it as a vision predominantly in time or in space than when we see it in both equally, as we normally do. There are moments when we appear to catch a glimpse of all our actions, their causes, their results, their whole sequence through time, in one flash. There are others, when we are conscious that all our conduct is typical, that we respond as other people do, and that our feelings and our conduct are like theirs. These two experiences are distinguished from the normal in seeming more intense and in seeming more complete. They are the moments which are given permanence in the dramatic and the character novel respectively; they are perfectly distinct; we can never have them at the same time. They are more complete than our other moments, because we can see life in perspective, we can see it whole, with a design and a significance, seeing it in time, or seeing it in space, but not seeing it in both at the same moment. In the mere process of living we see life in this way—that is, without perspective. For in our daily life the facts of time and space are equally immediate, and all that we are conscious of is a flux, with a significant crystallisation here and there, but without a design. The moment of æsthetic vision lifts us out of the flux. "Instead of a continuous, endless scene, in which the eye is caught in a thousand directions at once, with nothing to hold it to a fixed centre, the landscape that opens before us is whole and single; it has passed through an imagination, it has shed its irrelevancy, and is compact with its own meaning." [1]

We come now to a third division only less important than these two; one, moreover, which includes what many people consider the greatest novel ever written. Scattering all our generalisations, *War and Peace* seems to give a comprehensive picture of life both in time and space, and in spite of that to achieve universality. Obviously a theory of the novel which does not find a place for *War and Peace* is untenable. Nor does it better things to call the story two or several novels, as Mr Percy Lubbock has done, not with-

[1] *The Craft of Fiction*, by Percy Lubbock (Scribner).

out justice; for the problem would still remain to fit these into our scheme. In both or in all of them the story would still seem to be advancing in time and exploring space.

But though formidable, the problem is not unanswerable. Space and time seem equally real in *War and Peace*; but in fact its action takes place in time and time alone. The houses, the drawing-rooms, the streets, the country estates, are evoked, it is true, as definite and recognisable as those in *Vanity Fair*; but they have not the immutability of Russell Square and Queen's Crawley; they alter, like the characters, and altering become mere aspects of time. At the start they are simply places where people live, like the scenes in *Vanity Fair*; but presently they become places where people have lived, like the village which Rip Van Winkle returned to after his long sleep. Tolstoy's aim in *War and Peace* is not the same as Thackeray's, to show a static representation of society in which people behave in a uniform way and in a generalised present; it is, I quote Mr Percy Lubbock, "to enact the cycle of birth and growth, death and birth again." The characters, he goes on, "illustrate the story that is the same always and everywhere"; but in that story time is everything; it is more even than it is in the dramatic novel. For in the dramatic novel the action is a single action, and it may appear therefore against a changeless background; but here, in the perpetual succession of actions following one another, even the background must be subject to change. The universal behind the particular in the dramatic novel is the earth, or, if one likes, the cosmos; it is a stage. The universal behind the particular in *War and Peace* is change itself; it is a process. In the first the particular is set sharply against the universal; in the second it is not so much an image as a part of it, and finally melts into it. "The cycle of birth and growth, death and birth again," can neither be called merely particular, nor simply universal. It is both, because it is human life.

In *War and Peace*, then, human life is not set against fate or society, but against human life in perpetual change. It is not a particular image of a general law; it is particular and general at the same time; it is typical rather than symbolical. We cannot think of the dramatic novel without thinking of the idea of Fate, an abstraction, or of the character novel without thinking of society, another abstraction. But the only abstraction, the only point of general reference in *War and Peace* is "life," or more comprehensively, change. It is the most inclusive, it is also the vaguest, of the three.

For the novelist, as we have seen, fate is an organising conception of the first power, and society an organising conception of secondary power. Life or change, however, is hardly an organising conception at all; as it is comprehensive it includes everything; and we shall find that the structure of the kind of novel of which *War and Peace* is the greatest example is the loosest of the three. This kind of novel I shall call the chronicle. Its action is almost accidental, but we shall find later that all the events happen within a perfectly rigid framework. A strict framework, an arbitrary and careless progression; both of these, we shall find, are necessary to the chronicle as an æsthetic form. Without the first it would be shapeless; without the second it would be lifeless. The one gives it its universal, the other its particular reality. As Time, however, is the main ground of the chronicle, so each of those two planes of the plot is a separate aspect of Time. They may be called Time as absolute process, and Time as accidental manifestation.

We have already pointed out the primacy of the sense of time in the dramatic novel. In it Time is incarnated and articulated in the characters; its speed therefore is psychological, determined by the slowness or rapidity of the action. Turning to *War and Peace*, we shall find that there Time is not so much articulated as generalised and averaged. Its speed is not determined by the intensity of the action; it has, on the contrary, a cold and deadly regularity, which is external to the characters and unaffected by them. The characters grow, or grow old. The emphasis is on that; on the fact that they are twenty now, that they will be thirty, then forty, then fifty, and that in essential respects they will then be like everybody else at twenty, thirty, forty, and fifty. We watch the change taking place within Catherine and Heathcliff; it is as if in them Time were dramatised. They change in a particular direction and for specific causes, and it is the strict concatenation of those causes that makes the change inevitable. Change in *War and Peace*, on the other hand, is primarily general, and its inevitability consists in its generality. It is not organic with the action, now rapid, now almost stationary, coinciding with the movement of the passions and the feelings; it follows the remote astronomical course which for mankind determines time's measurement; it is regular, arithmetical, and in a sense inhuman and featureless. It has one kind of necessity, that of increasing the ages of all the characters arithmetically, of continuing to change them at a uniform rate without paying attention to their desires or their plans. But everything except its own progression is indifferent to it. Natasha, Nicholas, and Prince Peter in *War and Peace* pass through sufferings which they feel at the time they cannot survive; nevertheless Tolstoyan time carries them indifferently on, as if experience did not matter, through a typical youth and maturity to a typical middle-age. Therefore—this is the other aspect of time seen in this way—everything may happen; and everything does happen. The action on the human plane does not unfold inevitably; we do not see a drama contained within itself and building itself up on its own consequences; we see life in all its variety of accidents and inventions, marked off here and there by certain very important milestones, inscribed with different figures which designate the march of an external and universal process. This process, which is the framework of the action, is empty seen in one way, and seen in another contains all that is possible; it is accident and law, confusion and meaning, everything and nothing.

In the dramatic novel, as we saw, the characters are revealed by time; in the chronicle too, they are revealed by time, but here the revelation follows a different path. To the chronicler describing a number of lives from birth to death, ten, twenty, thirty, forty, fifty, are critical stages, poignant categories of reality, and that because the single life is the unit, and each halting-place takes the character farther from its beginning or gives a nearer view of its end. A young man, an old man: when we are in the mood of the chronicler these simple classifications have all the pathos of life and change. But if we are thinking of a complex of relationships which must be resolved, they fall into a secondary place. So to the dramatic novelist time reckoned in this way has not the same significance. There is one point in *Wuthering Heights* where we are told, as if by chance, that Heathcliff is twenty-seven. Here, after a period of intense experience, in which time has been pure inward reality, the arithmetical, external aspect of time is suddenly and prosaically recognised, and it is as if the characters had awakened from a dream. So this almost reassuring ordinary fact has an unexpectedly pathetic effect, the mere recognition of it seeming to draw Heathcliff from the more profound tides in which the action was moving, and to set him down in his diurnal surroundings, a pitiable and ordinary human being. It has the effect for an instant—so great is the power of suggestion—of making us think of Heathcliff as a man who will soon be thirty, and may conceivably live to a ripe old age; and we forget—in this pause—the destiny towards which we know, with another part of our mind, that he is moving. It is destiny, its foreknowledge and its approach, that measures time in the dramatic novel; and when destiny falls time ends —the problem has been resolved. But in the chronicle time is not measured by human happenings, no matter how important; it is; and it continues to exist unchanged after its story has been told, still as regular in its movement, still as rich in accident and in the multitudes of figures it will discover. So we find Mr Lubbock saying of *War and Peace* that "there is no perceptible horizon, no hard line between the life in the book and the life beyond it. The communication between the men and women of the story and the rest of the world is unchecked. It is impossible to say of Peter and Andrew and Nicholas that they inhabit 'a world of their own,' as the people in a story-book so often appear to do; they inhabit *our* world, like everybody else." When we have closed *War and Peace*, in other words, we feel that time "goes on." The process, ten, twenty, thirty, forty, fifty, and all the people by means of whose lives we count it, remain in our minds and in the world. "The cycle of birth and growth, death and birth again"; this has been the pattern of the story; but this is the pattern of life too. So that, finished, the chronicle releases an echo which wanders in larger spaces than those in which it has just been confined,

spaces, moreover, which repeat on an unimagin-
ably vaster scale the proportions of their original,
and respond to the same tones. Tolstoy describes
only a few generations, but the emphasis of his
imagination makes the endless cycle of generations
unroll in our imagination; and we see human life
as birth, growth, and decay, a process perpetually
repeated. This then is the framework, ideal and
actual, of the chronicle; its framework of universality.

But at the same time, within this process of
birth, growth and decay, as its content, are all the
diverse manifestations of life, everything that can
happen; and it is these that make up the particular
incidents in the chronicle; that fill and animate
it. Here, too, as in the dramatic novel, variety is
set against uniformity, freedom against necessity.
If one is overstressed in the chronicle, the story
will be untrue. If one is omitted, the story will
not be a work of imagination at all.

To bring out as clearly as possible the difference
between the sense of time in the dramatic novel
and the chronicle, I shall restate it now in another
way. Time in the dramatic novel is internal; its
movement is the movement of the figures; change,

fate, character, are all condensed into one action; and with its resolution there comes a pause in which time seems to stand still; the arena is left vacant. In the chronicle, on the other hand, time is external; it is not seized subjectively and humanly in the minds of the characters; it is seen from a fixed Newtonian point outside. It flows past the beholder; it flows over and through the figures he evokes. Instead of narrowing to a point, the point fixed by passion, or fear, or fate in the dramatic novel, it stretches away indefinitely, running with a scarcely perceptible check over all the barriers which might have marked its end. The figures who appear and disappear in this vast cycle of recurring movement may be involved in tragedies like that of Catherine and Heathcliff; but these will rarely be resolved, and if they are, the immense stretches of time called up will give the resolution a lesser significance, and make it merely one of the accidents of time. The characters in the dramatic novel, as we have seen, are set on an isolated stage, where the conflict between them can be worked out finally, where everything, therefore, is cause, effect, destiny. But take away the barriers which hedge in the drama; expand the stage until we see, instead of an isolated action, "the cycle of birth and growth, death and birth again," and what had been grasped before as absolute will be seen now as relative.

It is the unavoidable relativity of action in the chronicle, perhaps, that makes Mr Lubbock ask, writing of *War and Peace*: "But the meaning, the import, what I should like to call the moral of it all—what of that? Tolstoy has shown us a certain length of time's journey, but to what end has he shown it?" Yet it was surely an adequate feat to evoke for us an image of the cycle of recurring life, and what Mr Lubbock intends by "the meaning" of the book surely lies in that. If he wanted a different meaning, the meaning of *Wuthering Heights* or of *Vanity Fair*, obviously he was wanting something unreasonable. To see life over a long stretch of time, to take away irremediably the urgency of the present, is to change everything and to lose certain things. The tragic becomes the pathetic as it recedes in the back-flow of change; and it can never be the tragic at all so long as the writer knows to the point of conviction that it will recede, and that something else will take its place. When the immediacy and finality of the present is taken away from a happening, the sense of tragedy has been taken from it as well; there is, however, something left, with a relative but not an absolute power of moving us. There is not a catharsis, if that is what Mr Lubbock wanted; but there is this something else, and its total effect may be sufficient to recompense us for that absence. By virtue of its wider sweep the chronicle is not of course more "true" than the dramatic novel with its strict limitations. In no form that the imagination takes can human life be absolutely presented. The three divisions of the novel I have been trying to distinguish are merely three modes of presentation, none of them more valid by any objectively discoverable standard than the others.

This, then, is the respect in which the structure of the chronicle differs from that of the dramatic novel. The plot of the latter is a strict and logical development, that of the former a loose concatenation of episodes bound within a rigid external progression, which is time as it is reckoned by the human mind. This cosmic progression gives a different value to all the particular happenings, making the tragic pathetic, the inevitable accidental, the final relative, and doing this naturally and inevitably.

But if an additional practical reason should be wanted for the accidental appearance of the action in the chronicle, it may be found in the fact that the progress of time itself is so certain that only by episodic treatment can chance, uncertainty, freedom come in, holding the balance, and making the picture true. The change in Heathcliff's character, as it is not a change wrought by astronomical time, and is not compelled to keep pace with an empty and mechanical progression, can be explained by specific things he has done and suffered; the change is inevitable, in other words, without being lifelessly necessitated. But the development of Nicholas Rostoff between the ages of ten and twenty *is* predominantly a development wrought by astronomical time; accordingly it cannot be explained by specific things, but only by all the things which time might bring forth, all the things, in other words, which a youth is likely to do, think, and suffer in the interval. Therefore the novelist must describe a sufficient number and variety of these, and that, indeed, is all he need do. He must explain the change by filling in roughly the stretch of time in which it was taking place. To obtain variety, however, he will have to be as untrammelled by a strictly developing plot as the character novelist. He will not build up an action; he will fill in a picture, but this picture, unlike that of the character novelist, will change as he goes on. The figures will remain the same; but their appearance, the colour of their hair, their thoughts, their affections will continue to alter until the final alteration comes. And unlike the changes in the dramatic novel, these changes will be unexpected rather than accounted for. They will go on silently and unregarded, and only when they have taken place will someone, Nicholas or Natasha, awaken and exclaim, How changed I am! not knowing how this could have happened. In such moments as these, when the tramp of time marching behind the action is most clearly heard, all that the characters have done will seem accidental even to themselves, and by no scanning of it will they discover how they came to the point where they stand. It is the apparent waywardness of the action which produces those effects, probably the most profound the chronicle can evoke. During the ordinary tenor of the story time is silent, and the action flows on as a single wandering melody; but here the two movements meet in one chord; the echo dies away, the melody flows on again, changed a little; the chord is struck again. I have called the periods ten, twenty, thirty, forty, and so on. These, of course, are arbitrary divisions, and chosen only to emphasise the regularity of the movement of time in the chronicle. The chord may be struck, astronomical time may manifest itself openly, at the lapse of any period; the march of time, in any case, will not be affected.

The action of the chronicle, then, must be accidental; and in nothing can its arbitrariness be seen more fully than in the way it disposes of human life. In the dramatic novel the characters, to use Nietzsche's phrase, "die at the right time." Captain Ahab, Michael Henchard, Catherine Earnshaw make their exits at the moment which fate has for long prepared for them. But Prince Andrew is snuffed out accidentally, at the time when he is planning his future and resolving how he will live. Here Mr Lubbock's query comes in with peculiar force: "But the meaning, the import, what I should like to call the moral of it all—what of that?" If human will and prevision have any meaning, then it seems to be denied in the sudden taking off of Prince Andrew. Yet life had meaning for Tolstoy, and indeed behind the terrible inconsequence of Prince Andrew's death we are made to feel, if somewhat vaguely, that Tolstoy apprehended, or was trying to apprehend, the presence of a law to which this crushing out of meaning in a single life was perhaps necessary. What he apprehended was the law of fate in the chronicle; and this in essence is merely another aspect of arithmetical time, which contains everything—life, death, realisation, defeat; which contains them hypothetically in fixed and therefore in just proportions; but which releases them at its own predetermined moment, as it irrevocably unrolls. This fate is unknowable; it is apprehended by faith, not shown; transcendental, not immanent. It deals out every favour and every punishment, but on its own terms, in accordance with its own laws, and in a manner which seems to mankind now just and now unjust. In the dramatic novel fate is visible; we see it unfolding in the world, on which beats for the time being a more intense light than that of ordinary day; and because we see it manifested we understand it and acquiesce in it. In the chronicle, on the contrary, while the human world is clear and immediate, fate remains a mystery, and we can only submit to its unknowable laws by an act of faith. The chronicler's conception of fate, therefore, and especially in earlier times, has often been religious. This power which deals out, as if from a hidden world, adventure, pain, labour, pleasure, death, has awakened awe and demanded propitiation, or resignation, or acceptance; and perhaps at one time created the specific gods to whom these could be offered. The great antique chronicles, such as the story of David and The Odyssey, are religious—or at least what we now conveniently call religious—in their conception of fate. Mankind's capacity for "a willing suspension of disbelief," however, seems to be weakening; the conception of fate in *War and Peace*, or, to take a modern instance, *The Old Wives' Tale*, is but a shadow of what it was in the story of David; but a tincture of religious feeling nevertheless

remains in it. The belief in the efficacy of propitiation has gone, but the belief in something
beyond the accidental movement of human life
has remained, and with it that willing suspension
of disbelief which we call resignation or acceptance.
This, as a residue of religious feeling, will be found
in all examples of the chronicle, good or bad, for
no image of "the cycle of birth and growth, death
and birth again," can do other than imply it,
except at the expense of lacking any significance
at all. The dramatic novelist, on the other hand,
accepts a fate that is manifest in the world; and
this particular kind of faith is not required of him.
He sees the action as cause and effect; the chronicler sees it as human accident against transcendental law, both expressing one reality, but
moving on different planes. And as to the former
cause and effect must have both an interior and
an external reality if it is not to be merely
mechanical; so to the latter those two aspects
must be emphasised with equal force if they are
not to be meaningless. The known attribute of
the unseen fate—its regular progression—must
be rigidly held; the rest must be given as an
image of all that is conceivable.

In introducing, to some it will appear irrelevantly, the concepts of Time, Space, and Causality into a work of criticism, I may appear to have forgotten all the æsthetic canons, and to be erecting arbitrary and fanciful standards. If this is thought to be so, the only reply I can make is that in trying to find the reasons for the apparently arbitrary limitations of certain forms of the novel, I was driven back at last to the limitations of our vision of the world. We see things in terms of Time, Space, and Causality; and only the Supreme Being, Kant affirmed, can see the whole unity from beginning to end. Yet the imagination desires to see the whole unity, or an image of it; and it seems that that image can only be conceived when the imagination accepts certain limitations, or finds itself spontaneously working within them. If the matter could be pursued to the end, then I hold that it would be found that those limitations determine the principle of structure in the various types of imaginative creation; in the dramatic novel, for example, the character novel, and the chronicle. I do not claim that these are the only possible or the only existent forms of imaginative vision or of the novel; or that, subjected to limitations which we cannot anticipate at present, the imagination may not yet discover new modes. But they are at least three very salient and very important forms, with a long tradition and, as a corollary, a persistent reality. Their limitations, as I have tried to trace them, are legitimate ones, not the limitations of any particular author, but of the human mind. This mind, trying to see life whole, has to narrow its focus, or instinctively does so; it renounces in order to gain; it withdraws itself to one remove from life that it may see life clearly. This withdrawal, this escape, is by the criteria of living an arbitrary act, and brings with it a long train of arbitrary effects, the "limitations" which we have been considering. But it is at the same time a creative act, justified not only negatively by necessity, but positively in the evocation of a world which could not have been born in any other way.

V

THE PERIOD NOVEL AND LATER DEVELOPMENTS

THE chronicle is the ruling convention of the novel at present: the most consistently practised, the most highly thought of. Such stories as *Sons and Lovers*, *A Portrait of the Artist as a Young Man*, and *Jacob's Room* are in their different ways in the tradition; and so are most of the works of Mr Compton Mackenzie, Mr Walpole, and Mr Beresford, and a great number of other writers of respectable talent. The three novels just mentioned are perhaps the best chronicles that have appeared in recent years. All the same, the most striking achievements of the contemporary novel lie outside the chronicle, and we shall have to consider these more fully. But first it is necessary to deal with a kind of novel which has many superficial resemblances to the chronicle, which a generation ago had an immense vitality, but which now seems to be sinking into a decline.

It is the kind of novel which is represented most brilliantly by the Clayhanger trilogy, *The Forsyte Saga*, *The New Macchiavelli*, and Mr Dreiser's records of American life. The immediate aim of all these is essentially different from that of the novels we have been considering up to now. It is less ambitious, less comprehensive; more immediate, more utilitarian. This kind of novel is not audacious enough to attempt a picture of society valid for all time; its object is more modest and specific, to show us a section of contemporary society, and to show it, moreover, in transition. To emphasise the difference between this period novel and the chronicle, I shall have to cite Tolstoy again. Tolstoy was not concerned with the evolution of society, as Mr Lubbock, whom I must quote once more, justly notes. Speaking of the characters in *War and Peace*, he says: "It does not matter, it does not affect the drama, that they are men and women of a certain race and century, soldiers, politicians, princes, Russians in an age of crisis; such they are, with all the circumstances of their time and place about them, but such they are in secondary fashion, it is what they happen to be. . . . It is laid upon them primarily to enact the cycle of birth and growth, death and birth again. They illustrate the story that is the same always and everywhere, and the tumult of the dawning century to which they are born is an accident." The latter part of this is true, of course, not only of *War and Peace*, but of every true work of imagination that has ever been written. But it is true hardly at all of *The New Macchiavelli*, and it is true only in part of the Clayhanger trilogy and *The Forsyte Saga*. Tolstoy's aim was æsthetic; Mr Galsworthy's and Mr Wells's is not. These authors rise into the world of imagination occasionally, it is true, but only in disregard of their aim, not in pursuance of it. The period novel as a form differs from the chronicle, therefore, not merely in degree of excellence, but in kind. It does not try to show us human truth valid for all time; it is content with a society at a particular stage of transition, and characters which are only true in so far as they are representative of that society. It makes everything particular, relative and historical. It does not see life with the universalising imagination, but with the busy, informing eye, aided by the theorising intelligence.

The bondage of the novel to period has naturally degraded it. Mr Bennett's and Mr Wells's many descriptions of the devices which have changed modern life are of course interesting, and these inventions are important in their sphere; but no one could imagine their being given any consequence in a novel moving at the imaginative tension of *War and Peace*, or even of *Barchester Towers*. In a recent novel a lady makes one of her characters clatter up to take part in a very poignant scene in a noisy motor car. Motor cars had just come in, and this was her way of letting the reader know, and of insisting that society was evolving!

The bondage of the novel to period has degraded it. But it also insensibly falsified for a time the standards of criticism, and they still show its influence. Exactitude of contemporary detail became more important than exactitude of imagination. Novelists prided themselves particularly on the labour they spent on documenting their subjects, as if the ardours of the imagination were in comparison frivolous and easy,

exacting no energy. They need only have cast
a glance over the history of the novel to see how
absurd were their standards. Whether the period
detail in *Old Mortality*, *Tom Jones*, *Wuthering
Heights*, *Vanity Fair*, or *La Cousine Bette* is historically correct or not does not matter now to any-
body but literary pedants. And that the period
detail in the Clayhanger trilogy or *The Forsyte
Saga* is historically true will not matter in another
twenty years; indeed, it has almost ceased to
matter already. For the period novel is dying
out; it is already outmoded; and the best work
in contemporary fiction is in a different style.

One of the most illuminating diagnoses of the
period novel has been written by the French
critic M. Ramon Fernandez in his volume of
essays, *Messages*. He prefaces his essay on Balzac
with a distinction between the novel, as a pure
æsthetic form, and what he calls the *récit*; but
though the *récit* designates a much bigger class
than the period novel, his observations apply so
exactly to the latter, that I can quote them almost
without qualification. "This is how one might
distinguish the novel from the recital," he says.
"*The novel is the representation of events which take*

place in time, a representation submitted to the conditions of apparition and development of these events. The recital is the presentation of events which have taken place, and of which the reproduction is regulated by the narrator in conformity with the laws of exposition and persuasion. . . . The essential difference is then that the event of the novel *takes place*, whereas that of the recital *has taken place*, that the recital is ordered around a past and the novel in a present not verbal but psychological." [1] This is Mr Fernandez's main generalisation. I would like to quote all that he says about it, but I shall have to limit myself to the paragraphs which apply particularly to the period novel.

"Treating of the past, of the lived, of the terminated," he says, "the recital is not obliged to respect the characters, or the actual and living development of a scene or of a psychic complex; it may substitute for them, in fact most often it does substitute for them, a mode of presentation nearer, on the one hand, to reasoning and the intellectual laws of combination, and on the other

[1] *Messages,* Ramon Fernandez. Librairie Gallimard, Paris. Also translated by Montgomery Belgion. (Harcourt, Brace.) I have used Mr. Belgion's translation.

hand to painting and the general laws of description. For, as soon as one ceases to express an actual life carrying along belief by its very unrolling in time, as soon as one wants to recount, give an account of, make known, one willingly has recourse to the most proper means of demonstrating, of convincing, and one seeks for the reasons for acts, and the intelligent continuity of sentiments, which is not often to be mistaken for their living continuity. . . . Thus, *the recital tends to the substitution of an order of conceptual exposition for the order of living production, and of rational proofs for æsthetic proofs.*" After a long and interesting elaboration of this thesis he concludes: "In the novel the idea is suggested by the concrete representation which reveals it as it were transparently; in the recital this representation is determined by the idea, or at least exhibited according to an ideal and abstract line."

These generalisations may quite easily, I think, be fitted to the period novel. Take M. Fernandez's last observation first, and remark how exquisitely it defines the difference between *Vanity Fair* and *The New Macchiavelli*, or *The Forsyte Saga*. All three are pictures of society; the idea of all three, to use M. Fernandez's term, is the idea of society; but in *Vanity Fair* that idea is "suggested by the concrete representation," and is revealed by it "as it were transparently"; whereas in *The New Macchiavelli* and *The Forsyte Saga* "the representation is determined by the idea, or at least exhibited according to an ideal and abstract line." To Mr Wells and Mr Galsworthy society is essentially an abstract conception, not an imaginative reality; they do not recreate society, therefore, in their novels; they merely illustrate it, or rather their ideas about it. Thackeray sets his characters going, he exhibits them continuously "in a present not verbal but psychological," and at the end a picture of society has sprung up before our eyes. But to Mr Wells and Mr Galsworthy society is there full grown as an idea at the beginning; it is not created by the characters, rather it creates them; but at the same time it is always beyond them, exists as a thing in itself, and cannot be adumbrated completely except by employing the arts of "exposition and persuasion." This also means, to refer to M. Fernandez again, that psychologically the events "have taken place" already; the thing which explains them, the idea of society, being there before they had begun to exist. These events and these characters are not seized as realities in themselves, in other words, but are used as illustrations of a reality which eternally remains outside and is never incarnated. At moments Mr Wells and Mr Galsworthy forget the idea, and then they are novelists in the beaten track, like Thackeray or Dickens. But we are considering the form they have used and upheld, and to this form all the bad things that M. Fernandez says about the *récit* are clearly applicable. It is not essentially an æsthetic form, and its practicians do not attain universality by obeying its laws, but by disregarding them. It lays importance on elements which to a later age will have but an historical interest, the atmosphere of a special period or a particular environment.

For the imaginative writer can draw a picture of society; but only an historian can reconstruct a particular society or show us a society in evolution; and the period novel is really a spurious kind of history which occasionally breaks into fiction. It is never both at the same time; when it is of help to the social student it is worthless for the critic, and *vice versa*. It is stuck together, not created. In the simplest primitive legend there is more of the philosophical quality of imagination than in this form once so highly considered.

A great deal more might be said about the period novel, but this must serve in a short survey of the major forms, to which it does not belong. The two outstanding works of prose fiction of the present age are almost certainly *A la recherche du temps perdu* and *Ulysses*. Neither is in the reigning tradition of the chronicle; and both have been claimed as new forms. For contemporary reasons they demand attention.

The first has been called, and clearly with justice, a great work. But it is exactly enough what it is entitled, an investigation and recreation of past scenes. It has more resemblance in form and spirit to Thackeray than to Tolstoy. Proust's starting-point, like Thackeray's, is the present, and his work is given unity, as Thackeray's was, by the perspective of the present, which puts all the past in its place and composes it into a picture. But in this pictured, spatial past Proust does not follow the beaten track, like Thackeray; he takes

any and every way, moves backwards and forwards
as he likes, led not by the story, but by a psychological movement behind it, into which the various
scenes fit as into a changing mosaic. It is this
psychological movement that gives unity, a sort
of unity at one remove, to *A la recherche du temps
perdu*. Superficially it is a collection of character
and dramatic novels interwoven with one another;
but more essentially it is an unique example of
the dramatic novel, with an end, not in the
external action, but in the author's mind: the
end of a search rather than of a conflict. Removed
from their context certain sections of *A la recherche
du temps perdu* might simply pass as character
novels; but the writing of a character novel may
be conceived as a dramatic action in itself, and
it is this that Proust has staged on another plane
of imagination and in the background of his great
work. Actually he never succeeded in separating
his work from himself and sending it out as an
independent entity; the navel string was never
cut; but by a happy stroke of genius he managed
to turn this misfortune into an advantage. He
gives us not only the results of his imagination,
but the processes as well, and on top of that the

effect of those processes on himself, and in addition his reflections on those effects. What we are shown, therefore, is not merely a number of novels, but the mind which conceives them, and in its struggle with them. Of Proust's work one might say more legitimately than of André Gide's *Les Faux Monnayeurs* that it is "a novel about a novelist writing a novel." The form was legitimate, for it suited Proust's unique genius; but it is questionable whether it could ever be used by anyone else.

The position of *Ulysses* is somewhat different. The claim has been made for it that it has revolutionised prose fiction, and that it is not a novel at all, but the end of the novel and the beginning of something else. If the sphere of the character novel is space, the sphere of the dramatic novel time, then, so it has been suggested, that of *Ulysses* is a sort of space-time. Its intention is not to show a pattern of society or of fate, but to catch the flux as it moves. Characters, humours, and passions come in, but these are means for defining the feeling of time and space perpetually changing.

Ulysses is a work of extraordinary literary

virtuosity, and some of its technical innovations are striking; but in structure it is not revolutionary. Its faults are obvious: its design is arbitrary, its development feeble, its unity questionable. Like *War and Peace*, it begins at an arbitrary point, but it has a fault peculiar to itself: it could end as suitably as it does at a dozen places. The first chapter, the first two chapters, the second and third, the fifth, the last: all these sections have as much unity, and the same kind of unity, as the whole. *Ulysses* proceeds by agglomeration, not by development. The plan which Mr Joyce professes to read into it is purely contingent and theoretical, not the animating principle of the whole, but a key which we may apply to it if we like. The symbolism of *Ulysses*, however, is hardly to be taken seriously; though at first sight it may appear to have the advantage of giving an additional significance to the book, on reflection it can only convince us that its significance is insufficient. In any case, *Ulysses* will inevitably be judged as it stands. Its effect as a work of imagination is all it will be able to rely upon, and the author's intentions or theories will have no power to influence the reader.

Mr Joyce's insistence on the symbolical framework of the book is then a confession that it is
formless in itself. The Ulyssian plot, in that
case, is simply a framework intended to keep the
story's formlessness within bounds, an external
mould to prevent the theme from running into
complete chaos. But the restraints being external,
the shapelessness being present, the reader is most
immediately affected by that. Not knowing that
Stephen is Telemachus and Bloom Odysseus, or
not caring much if he does, he will not see any
reason why the story should begin precisely where
it begins or end just where it ends.

All this has some truth, yet his criticism will
have less validity than it seems. In spite of its
arbitrary construction, *Ulysses* has somewhat the
same kind of congruity as a rambling novel of
character; it portrays a society, and its justification is that it goes on until the picture is complete.
Thackeray kept his picture expanding by skilful
transitions from incident to incident; Mr Joyce
uses no transitions at all; he paints a solid block
of his canvas, and when it is done goes on to
another. The result is that Thackeray's picture,
growing continuously, is complete and indivisible,

whereas Mr Joyce's is a succession of parts, done in different styles, making up a whole which is loose and redundant, but not unimpressive.

It must have been his attempt to give an impression of the flux that compelled him to adopt such a clumsy structure. To record the floating thoughts of one man for a day would provide matter for a library. To apply the same method to a number of characters makes all construction impossible. Yet Mr Joyce obviously wished, while doing this as far as possible, to draw a picture of Dublin life as well, and he had therefore to rely upon a number of hours picked out from the twenty-four, in which his characters might see the town from different aspects. The plan is clumsy, but it is imposed by his attempt to catch the flux. He does not, moreover, catch the flux. Bloom's floating fancies tell us a great deal about himself, but they do not make time appear to flow; everything in *Ulysses*, on the contrary, has an almost stagnant stillness; time remains stationary through each scene until Mr Joyce is ready to go on to the next. The reason for this is that floating thoughts which follow no progression, as they omit the idea of causality, are incapable of suggesting the idea of time. Our minds marshal them into a list of qualities which make up the character of Bloom, not into a series of states of mind following one another. We are interested in their nature, not in their order of succession; and so we see the figure of Bloom being built up where perhaps we were intended to see a movement. The flux has never been caught in a work of art; to catch it, indeed, would be to forgo that abstraction, that withdrawal to one remove from life, which is the condition, as we have seen, of creative imagination. In trying to catch it, Mr Joyce succeeds in doing something quite different.

As an attempt, then, to transcend the divisions of the novel, *Ulysses* is a failure. Setting out apparently to be a resumption of prose fiction and the beginning of a new form, it succeeds really in being a highly interesting variation of the character novel. Mediocre or meretricious where it tries to render a movement or describe a development, as for instance in the figure of Stephen Dedalus, it is admirable wherever it touches the static and the typical: in the character of Bloom, the conversations, the half-thoughts, the ruminations. These are almost clichés, as all static characters and all good comic dialogue tend to be. Bloom's ruminations are full of ideas which might serve as subjects for an essayist. The dialogue is an encyclopædia of the popular idioms of Dublin talk. Mr Joyce sees all his characters except the central one absolutely as the traditional character novelist might see them: Buck Mulligan, John Eglinton, A.E., the newspaper men, the priests, the topers, the men about town, the prostitutes, the soldiers. The book is a panoramic picture of Dublin, not an impression of the passing of a day. The flux coagulates into subject-matter for characters and scenes, into that and nothing more. The day is merely the frame of the picture. As one is needed, it serves well enough.

It is almost, indeed, as if an intention stronger than Mr Joyce's had turned what he set out to do into something else. The result, however, is of great interest. In a man of imaginative power the attempt to widen or break the traditional forms will have salutary effects, though it may bring him back to them again. Mr Joyce is one of the few contemporary writers who by an attempted revolution have infused new life into the novel of character. One has only to compare *Ulysses* with any current traditional novel of character to see that it is more real and more adequate.

The same may be said of Mrs Woolf's *Mrs Dalloway* and, with qualifications, of Mr Huxley's stories. Mrs Woolf has worked out a form of fine exactitude; Mr Huxley has improvised one from borrowed parts recast into a personal vehicle of expression. Both (I am thinking, however, of the author of *Mrs Dalloway*, not of *The Voyage Out*) are character novelists like Mr Joyce; their work is descriptive rather than dramatic; their vision is of scenes rather than of sequences. *Mrs Dalloway* is the most skilful spatial picture of life in contemporary literature. The relations which it brings out are horizontal, the relations between different characters or places, not those between cause and effect in time. Even the evocations of the past have a purely pictorial quality; they do not recall a different scene, rather they round out the present one; and each has the quality of this summer's day in London.

When we have mentioned Mr Joyce, Mrs

Woolf, and Mr Huxley, however, the list of contemporary English writers who have made any innovations of consequence in the structure of the novel is exhausted. Whether these innovating movements will succeed, what convention they will crystallise into, what new factors in social life or in the writer's vision of it or in contemporary thought and sensibility have led to them, are questions which it would be idle to pursue, for nobody knows anything about them. But *Ulysses* and *Mrs Dalloway* in their very different styles seem to be more in the pure æsthetic tradition of prose fiction than the work of the preceding generation, the generation of the period novel. The "idea" of the life they describe is, to return to M. Fernandez, "suggested by the concrete representation," and revealed "as it were transparently"; the picture is not "determined by the idea," nor even, in spite of Mr Joyce's notions, "exhibited according to an ideal or abstract line." These two novels are devious returns to the pure imaginative convention, and, in reacting against the period novel, unconsciously take their development from an earlier and traditional form.

VI

CONCLUSION

THE main object of the plot of the character novel, we agreed earlier, was to introduce and keep moving a variety of characters. That being so, however, this type of plot can only be justified as a major literary convention by proving that the characters it introduces have truth. This has not been done yet. We agreed that those characters were static, and that the object of the novelist justified this distortion of reality. But if they were not true in some sense as well, the distortion would be merely a clever device. Perhaps our advance to this question can best be made through certain observations of Mr E. M. Forster in his *Aspects of the Novel.*

To meet the new demands of a changing social order and of developing thought in the eighteenth century, the political economists invented the economic man. In the same way, and about the same time, the novel of character popularised the social man. The economic man is a pure abstraction, and in the social man, too, there is a touch of the abstract. He might be called the image which every man creates of himself, partly consciously, partly involuntarily, in adapting himself to society; the figure that he wants to make in the eyes of his circle, or the one that his character forces him to make, or partly the one and partly the other. Seen hastily, this social image might seem a façade merely; yet obviously it is an aspect of its possessor, even when it seems unlike him. It is not all of him, but it is true to him. It is the part of him which the novel of character sets in the foreground.

This is the type of character, one imagines, that Mr Forster calls flat, as against the round. "Flat characters," he says, "were called 'humours' in the seventeenth century, and are sometimes called types, and sometimes caricatures. In their purest form they are constructed round a single idea or quality: when there is more than one factor in them, we get the beginning of the curve towards the round. The really flat character can be expressed in one sentence, such as, 'I will never desert Mr Micawber.' There is Mrs Micawber —she says she won't desert Mr Micawber, she doesn't, and there she is." He points out the advantages possessed by flat characters: "they are easily recognised whenever they come in," and "easily remembered by the reader afterwards"; advantages which incidentally belong to people's social images of themselves, and to nothing else about them. He adds that "a serious or tragic flat character is apt to be a bore. Each time he enters crying 'Revenge!' or 'My heart bleeds for humanity!' or whatever his formula is, our hearts sink. One of the romances of a popular contemporary writer is constructed round a Sussex farmer, who says, 'I'll plough up that bit of gorse.' There is the farmer, there is the gorse; he says he'll plough it up, he does plough it up, but it is not like saying, 'I will never desert Mr Micawber,' because we are so bored by his consistency that we do not care whether he succeeds with the gorse or fails."

The explanation, however, is unsatisfactory, or rather is not an explanation at all. The question is why "I'll plough up that bit of gorse" should bore us by its consistency, and "I will never desert Mr Micawber" should not. And it is obviously because Mrs Micawber's formula comes out of her fictitious social image, and that this, though a cliché, reveals the real woman to us; whereas the Sussex farmer is intended to show us his heart, and shows us his social image instead, without the author's being aware of it. His formula is therefore false in its place, as Mrs Micawber's is true. "Revenge," "My heart bleeds for humanity," "I'll plough up that bit of gorse," are examples of involuntary humour; Mrs Micawber's sentence is not. That is the real difference between them.

Thus far Mr Forster's flat character corresponds to the typical static character of Dickens and Thackeray. But Mr Forster is obviously not much interested in it; he depreciates it, and he does it injustice by claiming certain flat characters as round. "The Countess in *Evan Harrington*," he says, "furnishes a good little example here. Let us compare our memories of her with our memories of Becky Sharp. We do not remember what the Countess did or what she passed through. What is clear is her figure and the formula that surrounds it, namely, 'Proud as we are of dear papa, we must conceal his memory.'   All her rich humour proceeds from this.   She is a flat character.   Becky is round.   She, too, is on the make, but she cannot be summed up in a single phrase, and we remember her in connection with the great scenes through which she passed, and as modified by those scenes—that is to say, we do not remember her so easily because she waxes and wanes and has facets like a human being." Yet how many people would agree with Mr Forster about Becky?   Dostoevsky's characters, he says, are round; so is Emma Bovary; and so, one imagines, are Catherine Earnshaw and Anna Karenina.   But compared with these Becky, though seriously conceived, though a masterpiece, is as flat as Mrs Micawber or Mr Pickwick, of whom Mr Forster says cleverly that "at any moment we may look at him edgeways and find him no thicker than a gramophone record."   Mr Forster, one imagines, was led a little astray by his test for flat characters.   Becky certainly cannot be expressed in a single formula; but she could be expressed in a number of formulæ; and her affinity consequently is with Mrs Micawber rather than with Anna Karenina.   She is a woman, yet as a French critic has complained, she is incapable either of passion or of love. Mr Forster's test for the round character, moreover, is its capacity for "surprising us in a convincing way" —an admirable test. "If it never surprises, it is flat. If it does not convince, it is a flat pretending to be round. It has the incalculability of life about it—life within the pages of a book." But Becky never surprises us enough to pose as a round character; and she is almost devoid of the chief incalculable factor in life, of passion, of sex.

To see the flat character in proportion, after Mr Forster's somewhat summary dismissal of it, perhaps the best thing we can do is to make a short list of some of the chief flat characters. The list would include Parson Adams (whom Mr Forster excludes, however), Partridge, Squire Western, Commodore Trunnion, Lismahago, Bailie Nicol Jarvie, Dandie Dinmont, Dugald Dalgetty, Mr Collins, Miss Bates, Becky Sharp, Captain Costigan, Major Pendennis, Joe Sedley, Pecksniff, Sam Weller, Dick Swiveller, Sairey Gamp, Quilp, Mrs Poyser, Mrs Proudie, Roy Richmond, Kipps, Mr Polly, and a host more whose names would fill pages. Take them all away, and we take away at least three-quarters of the figures in English fiction, as well as whole leagues of the England of the imagination, leaving only an intensely real but sparsely peopled area here and there—the Yorkshire moors, Wessex, George Douglas's Barbie. The flat character cannot be dismissed so easily, then. Having done so, indeed, Mr Forster feels that there is something wrong. "A novel that is at all complex," he remarks, "often requires flat people as well as round. . . . The case of Dickens is significant. Dickens' people are nearly all flat. . . . Nearly every one can be summed up in a sentence, and yet there is this wonderful feeling of human depth. Probably the immense vitality of Dickens causes his characters to vibrate a little, so that they borrow his life and seem to lead one of their own. . . . Part of the genius of Dickens is that he does use types and caricatures, people whom we recognise the instant they re-enter, and yet achieves effects that are not mechanical and a vision of humanity that is not shallow. Those who dislike Dickens have an excellent case. He ought to be bad. He is actually one of our big writers, and his immense success with types suggests that there may be more in flatness than the severer critics admit."

Or than Mr Forster will admit either. He tries to suggest that Dickens' characters are alive in spite of their flatness; their creator's immense vitality causes them "to vibrate a little, so that they borrow his life and seem to lead one of their own." But this is obviously true of any imagined figure; of Dmitri Karamazov or Father Goriot as certainly as of Pecksniff. The qualification has no meaning.

The mark of the pure character, we agreed in an earlier chapter, is that it is static; in other words, it "can be expressed in a single sentence," or, let us say, in a few sentences. The mark of the dramatic character is that it develops; it cannot therefore be expressed in a single sentence, or in a few sentences. The first, the pure character, or type, or humour, is flat, to adopt Mr Forster's classification; the second, the dramatic, developing figure, is round. So far all is clear. But the first, nevertheless, is capable of achieving "effects that are not mechanical and a vision of humanity that is not shallow." How is this?

The explanation is simple enough. The flat character, being flat, has two sides. All pure characters, formally, are in a sense artificial. They continue to repeat things *as if* they were true. Perhaps these things were once true; but they have long since ceased to have their first fresh conviction and have become habitual. Everybody reiterates certain sentiments half mechanically in this way, just as everybody repeats certain gestures, once spontaneous and passionate. It is this accumulation of habits, dictated by their natures or imposed by convention, that makes every human being the potential object of humour. The flat character is pre-eminently this incarnation of habit.

The dramatic figure is the opposite of the man of habit; he is the permanent exception. He breaks habit, or has it broken for him; he discovers the truth about himself, or in other words develops. He dramatises his real nature, where the flat character dramatises his second nature, or at best something in him which has been real but is so no longer. The utterance of the dramatic figure is therefore actually true, the utterance of the character symptomatic or symbolical.

A few instances will make clearer what is really a very obvious point. Here is the first:

MICHAEL HENCHARD'S WILL

That Elizabeth Jane Farfrae be not told of my death, or made to grieve on account of me.

& that I be not bury'd in consecrated ground.

& that no sexton be asked to toll the bell.

& that nobody be wished to see my dead body.

& that no murners walk behind me at my funeral.

& that no flours be planted on my grave.

& that no man remember me.

To this I put my name.

Here are the others:

"Eggs, even they have their moral. See how they come and go! Every pleasure is transitory. We can't even eat, long. If we indulge in harmless fluids, we get the dropsy; if in exciting liquids, we get drunk. What a soothing reflection is that!"

"As I must therefore conclude that you are not serious in your rejection of me, I shall choose to attribute it to your wish of increasing my love by suspense, according to the usual practice of elegant females."

"Cape Breton an island! wonderful!—show it me on the map. So it is, sure enough. My dear sir, you always bring us good news. I must go and tell the king that Cape Breton is an island."

The last quotation is from history, the others are from fiction. The difference between the first and the rest is, in any case, striking enough. Michael Henchard speaks from the heart, the others speak from their habitual selves; and the reader is quite well aware of it.

Mr Forster, however, writes as if the reader were not aware of it; as if the flat character were set there to deceive us, and the novelist himself did not see through to the other side. It is obvious that he could not have meant just this, yet some such assumption is at the back of his objection to the flat character. Mrs Micawber, of course, is always saying, "I will never desert Mr Micawber"; the Countess is always saying, "Proud as we are of dear papa, we must conceal his memory"; but that is not all. In a sense they both mean what they say; but there is sufficient hypocrisy in the manner to reveal with exactitude the real Mrs Micawber, the real Countess, whose features are printed on the other side of the record. Pecksniff, again, is always saying "What a soothing reflection is that!" He does not mean what he says at all; yet the façade suggests without further indication the real man which it appears to hide.   The dramatic novel is almost pure revelation, the character novel almost pure *suggestio falsi*.   Pecksniff is so completely given in the flat presentation that even if Dickens had never made him commit a mean or villainous act we should know he was a hypocrite.   The "unmasking" of flat characters (of which Dickens was so fond) is indeed always displeasing;   it makes a public announcement of an open secret. Dickens puts a term to Pecksniff's career;   he pulls off the mask;   and after that nothing remains, the substance has disappeared with the form. Thackeray was too intelligent to do such a thing often.   He rarely unmasked his characters, for he knew that they were unmasked the whole time.

This, then, is the reason why the flat character can be "summed up in a sentence, and yet there is this wonderful feeling of human depth."   But even in saying this Mr Forster again does an in-direct injustice to the flat character.   No doubt "I will never desert Mr Micawber" does bring Mrs Micawber before us once she is known;   but it could never have created her.   She lives for us because she says ever so many other things in character with "I will never desert Mr Micawber," because her sage reckoning of opportunities, her absurd optimism, and her ever-increasing family, are in consonance with it. The co-extensive truth and congruity of its attributes, indeed, makes the flat character no less remarkable as an imaginative creation than the round; it is not less true, it is only different. It shows us the real just underneath the habitual. If it did not show us the real it would be worthless, and there would be none of this "wonderful feeling of human depth." As it brings out this permanent contrast between the habitual and the real, however, it has to regard these as constant and immovable qualities. If a development were attempted, the contrast would lose its universality.

*   *   *   *

In separating prose fiction into three main divisions, the character novel, the dramatic novel, and the chronicle, it is obvious that we have been employing categories which apply to other forms of imaginative literature as well. This was inevitable, the laws of imagination being in some ways the same whether the writer's medium of expression be prose or poetry, whether he use the dramatic or the narrative form. In its

structure purely it is clear that the dramatic
novel has affinities with a large class; with the
whole of dramatic literature, both tragedy and
comedy, in the first place; with a great deal of
epic and saga literature as well. In formal drama
the qualities we have found in the dramatic novel
exist in their purity. The confinement to one
scene; the isolation of the characters; the unfolding development making towards an end; the
conflict; the *dénouement*; all are there as they
are in *Wuthering Heights* or in *The Return of the
Native*. "The confinement to one scene" may
be contested. In a play the scene changes, of
course, but the necessities of dramatic production
take away, it might be contended, all great
significance from the change; a blasted heath,
a cliff near Dover, a churchyard may be shown;
but what the eyes of the audience are fixed on
is a little lighted area where the same figures
appear and reappear until their conflict is worked
out. As in the dramatic novel, so here the scene
is always more than a particular scene; it is in
a sense symbolical. Whether the unities are
observed or not, in fact a sense of unity more
complete than any other kind of imaginative art

can attain, will be evoked in the concrete dramatic representation. This applies equally to tragedy and comedy. There is, as we have seen, affinities with both in the dramatic novel; in *Wuthering Heights* with tragedy, in *Pride and Prejudice* with comedy. The term dramatic, therefore, as applied to the novel, serves here quite accurately.

When we come to the character novel it is more difficult to discover relationships either to poetry or to dramatic literature. It seems, unlike the dramatic novel, to be a purely prose form. It is the only type of novel which would lose almost all its meaning if it were put on the stage. *Wuthering Heights*, *The Mayor of Casterbridge*, or *La Chartreuse de Parme* might conceivably be dramatised, for their movement could be concentrated into a number of developing scenes. But for the vast pictures of society in *Vanity Fair* and *Tom Jones* the stage is too narrow; their breadth — their distinguishing quality — would be lost. Nor in poetry can we find more than a fragment here and there that has much resemblance to the novel of character. The Prologue to *The Canterbury Tales*, a few satires, a brilliant interior like *The Jolly Beggars*, perhaps;

but nothing with the scope of *Tom Jones* or *Vanity Fair*; nothing which stands in the same relation to them as a great poetic tragedy to a great dramatic novel. On the other hand, the relation of the character novel to prose forms such as the Addisonian essay, to memoirs, letters, and the effusions which used to be called "characters," has often been noted. In its course the character novel has resumed all these minor traditions, however, and is now more important than all of them put together. The tradition of the dramatic novel fades back into that of the dramatic tragedy and the epic; into the greatest and oldest tradition in imaginative literature. Only at a very late stage has the novel of character become a central and major literary form.

The novel being a form of such mixed origin and such wide scope, any generalisations about it will apply only in certain particulars to other forms of imaginative literature. But that they should do so in part is all to the good. For the object of this argument is to show that the plot of the novel is as necessarily poetic or æsthetic as that of any other kind of imaginative creation. It will be an image of life, not a mere record of experience; but being an image it will inevitably observe the conditions which alone make the image complete and universal, and those, I have tried to show, reduce themselves to a representation of action predominantly in time or predominantly in space. Seeing life in time, or seeing it in space, the writer can work out the relations, the dynamic values, of his plot satisfactorily and to an end, and transform his vague and contingent sense of life into a positive image, an imaginative judgment. We have the same right to demand this imaginative judgment from a novel as we have to demand it from the poetic tragedy and the epic; for the novel is a form of art, like these, or it is nothing. If in most novels this transformation does not take place, then we know what to think; they are not literature, but merely confession. If again in the period novel the writer contents himself with drawing a picture of the contemporary changes in society, we know once more that this is not literature, but journalism. The influence of fashion is, of course, immense, the prestige of the accomplished fact difficult to undermine. The period novel is an accomplished fact; and only time perhaps will dislodge it from its position of grave consequence in literature, and relegate it to a humbler sphere. Criticism, however, should help as much as it can in the work. A great number of the wilder experiments in form recently must have sprung from a hopeless contemplation of the mediocrity of the conventions which the novel has observed for twenty years or so. If it could be proved that these conventions are not traditional but merely fashionable, the reaction against them might become more effective as well as less violent.

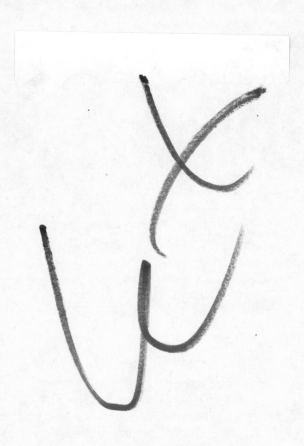